The Gift of Faith

BEVERly M. CoNyERS
To:

By the Author

The Power of Resurrection
The Wonder of Miracles
The Clarity of Visions

THE GIFT OF FAITH

MARGARET A. GRAHAM

1817

Harper & Row, Publishers, San Francisco

New York, Grand Rapids, Philadelphia, St. Louis
London, Singapore, Sydney, Tokyo, Toronto

FIRST EDITION

Library of Congress Cataloging-in-Publication Data

Graham, Margaret.
    The Gift of Faith/Margaret A. Graham.—1st ed.
      p.   cm.
    Includes bibliographical references.
    ISBN 0-06-063385-9 (pbk.)
     1. Bible stories, English.   2. Faith—Biblical teaching.
I. Title.
BS550. 2. G692 1989
234'.2—dc20   89-45523
                                           CIP

89 90 91 92 93 MCN 10 9 8 7 6 5 4 3 2 1

For
Jennie Graham Free
whose gift of faith has blessed many

Contents

Preface

Often biblical characters are relegated to the distant past as cardboard figures of a storybook world. There are reasons for this, none so valid as the contrast between the supposed immediacy of their interaction with God and our less than audible communication with him. And there is the characteristic restraint of the Holy Spirit in recording events without emphasis upon human interest and without appeal to the emotions. In short, the dramatic experiences of biblical people of faith, often in the midst of pain and conflict, were not accompanied by a sound track of drum rolls and trumpets heralding their valiancy.

It is important to strip away the cardboard images if we are to fully understand their struggles with the challenges of faith. Otherwise we may perceive that faith is instant, something that "just happens" without reference to what has gone before. Faith is never found in a vacuum. "Faith comes from hearing the message" (Rom. 10:17). On the surface it would seem that the centurion had little or no knowledge of the Scripture or of Jesus, yet he was credited by the Lord as having greater faith than those in Israel. From the few statements made about the centurion I have tried to recreate a situation in which he could have gained sufficient information for prompting his great statement of faith.

The genre of "faction," fiction based on fact, requires the author to set limitations on the imagination lest he or she be guilty of titillating prurient interest, misleading the reader, or falsifying facts. Particularly is this true in writing biblical stories. The sensitivity of an individual with an aversion for pictures of Christ because pictures may convey false notions about the Son of man is the sensitivity needed by the writer of biblical "faction." Reverence for the person of Christ, indeed for the Godhead, rules out physical description, the attributing of motives and attitudes, or gestures and expressions that would add to the scriptural revelation. The fiction in these stories is limited to other characters in the narrative and is used as a device for giving the reader historical, geographical, and societal facts. By fictionizing the account we can understand something of the pre-Flood civilization from the conversation of Noah's sons; we can "see" the civilization of Egypt through Joseph's eyes.

The fiction also helps us speculate about possible answers to questions inherent in the text. For instance, why did Paul wait days to cast out the demon in the girl at Philippi? His companions, Timothy, Silas, and Luke, offer "fictional" explanations.

The reason for adding details of a purely human interest is to help us feel what the man or woman of faith was feeling. I have given Rahab elderly parents, brothers in the militia, a widowed sister with three children, and another sister who is pregnant. The reason for this is to present a reality in which the reader better feels the anxiety of a woman responsible for the saving of her family in a dangerous situation.

In these biblical stories, with the exception of Gamaliel, who refused the gift of faith, all the men and women have extraordinary faith proved in a variety of circumstances. The commonality lies in their belief in the character of God, their belief in a content of truth, and the way they proved their faith by obedience and trust. They understood that "without faith it is impossible to please God, because anyone who comes to him must believe that he exists and that he rewards those who earnestly seek him" (Heb. 11:6). The gift of faith is for all of us.

Perhaps in the reading of these stories the sound track will be heard and the music of faith prove helpful in our own struggles.

Part I

Old Testament Examples

Noah

IN HOLY FEAR BUILT AN ARK . . .

Scripture: Heb. 11:7; Genesis 6–9

The long-horned buffalo pulling the cart that brought Noah up the mountain was blowing through his wide nostrils, tossing his head about, protesting the yoke. The water buffalo, accustomed to the delta and marsh lands of the plain, resisted the steep climb away from his natural workplace.

They were approaching a small herd of elephants, trained for the work of carrying logs, waiting for the trees to be felled. Noah enjoyed watching the elephants stripping bark with their tusks and using their trunks to put it into their mouths, filling their giant maws. A mother elephant called to her young, slapping her ears against her head. Noah smiled as she rumbled from somewhere deep within her cavernous bulk.

Arriving on the mountain slope, Noah gazed down upon the vast plain of the two rivers. Despite the haze he could see almost as far as the Shinar Plain where a bountiful harvest was waving in the wind and the wealthy homes of farmers and traders vied for prominence.

Lush vegetation bordered the Euphrates, a meandering black snake of water fed by streams and springs that tumbled down the wadis or ravines of the mountains. In turn, the river filled the canals crisscrossing the earth. Beyond the dikes was the Tigris, a tortuous, double-backing rush of water that was never quiet, never at rest. *So like the inhabitants of the land,* thought Noah.

Ever since invading bands poured in from the east, over-running the country, there had been no peace. These men of Nod did not come to conquer but to settle down, marry the women of Seth, and enjoy the benefits of the land. The horde of robust men, with their knowledge of village rule, cattle, ores, and music, were awesome in contrast to the God-fearing men of the river valley. Women were swept off their feet by the handsome rogues. Unfortunately, in one generation the children born of these unions had become warriors, wanting nothing more than to fight.

Noah turned his attention to the crew at work. Japheth, his youngest son, was working alongside the men, although he was not a timber man. The foreman gave the signal, and one of the younger men, equipped with an axe, shinnied up the tree to whack off the limbs. The rest of the men began laying brush along the path of the tree's fall to cushion the tree upon impact.

It was then that Noah overheard Japheth trying to justify his father to one of the young men. "Of course, things are different now than when he was our age, but he's no fool. I can vouch for his reason—it's as sound as ever. But my father is not ruled by reason."

"Ruled by a higher power, you'd say," responded Kenan, the young man.

"Not a power, Kenan, a person."

"Call it what you will; I, too, believe in God."

"You are not governed by him. You know no Sabbath, you lie, and you sleep with every woman you can."

"What harm's done? As for women, a man needs more than one. Don't think you won't know that after a few months, a few years with your new wife. No one else I know lives with but one wife the way your father and brothers, and now you, propose to do. You live in fear, Japheth, fear of the God you say you love."

"Fear God and you have nothing else to fear, Kenan."

"I fear nothing!" he shouted and swore. But in a few

minutes he admitted, "The wizard—I do fear the wizard. Such spells he casts!"

"The wizard?"

"A very wise man—head of the sorcerers' guild. He lives in the temple where the earth meets the sky."

"How can you believe such nonsense? There's no rhyme nor reason for fearing a wizard."

"Faith is all it takes, Japheth. I've seen the wizard, servant of the moon, and that's enough for me. You've never seen your God. You only trust the man who says he's seen or heard."

"You're wrong," Japheth argued. "We have the truth handed down to us by men who walked close to God."

"Tradition, that's what you have—only tradition."

"And you? You have more?"

"A great deal more. Our priest was taken into the fellowship of the gods and made acquainted with the secrets of heaven and earth."

"What secrets? Secrets that cause every human inclination to be only evil all the time? Secrets that have made your people savages, bloodthirsty, vile, and mad?"

"Secrets that liberated us from your God's restraints."

"There's no use arguing with you," Japheth stormed and walked away from him.

By afternoon the tree was felled, and the elephants began the work of getting it down the mountainside. With their trunks curled around the log, they lumbered two abreast down the slope.

Before dark the men and animals reached the Euphrates and dropped the logs in the holding pond where other trees floated. In the morning, the workers would tie the logs together and shove the makeshift raft into the current that would float it downstream.

Relieved of their burden, the elephants rushed down to the river, trumpeting the smell of water. Wading belly-deep into the river, they sucked up trunkfuls of water and let it stream in arcs over their backs.

Looking admiringly at the long, white tusks, Kenan boasted of his father's prowess as an elephant hunter. "My father, Maon, was the finest hunter in all the land of Nod. No man ever in a lifetime boasted more ivory than he. He taught other men how to hunt, how to set fires and encircle the elephants so that they die from breathing smoke or are burned to death. He was known as Maon the Great Ivory Master."

"That means he killed young elephants along with the old." Japheth said nothing more and busied himself with making camp.

Noah took up the matter. "Kenan, your father sinned. The Lord God has made us the lords of his Creation to take care of the beasts of the field and the fowls of the air. The slaughtering of elephant herds is cruel and wasteful, and God will judge anyone who kills wantonly."

Kenan sneered. "Lords of the Creation, indeed. Is that why you slaughter innocent lambs for your sacrifices?"

"We shed blood at the command of God to confess our sins and remember sin's penalty."

"Sin? What is sin? By whose standard? I'm as good as you." Yet, as he thought upon it, there showed in his face a consternation, and Japheth was about to seize the moment when they were interrupted.

A lookout, informed that river robbers were about, reported to Noah. "They're murderous, sir—they torture their victims and leave them maimed." Noah quickly appointed guards with dogs and posted them on the perimeters of the campsite.

When night fell and stars studded the sky, Kenan walked to the river's edge and bowed down to the starry heaven. A true believer in the fortune-telling of stars, the intensity of his devotion could not be more earnest if he were worshiping before the two pillars, the sacred observatories.

Japheth stopped watching him and busied himself with the campfire. "This is our last trip up the mountain, isn't it, Father?" he asked Noah. "Tomorrow we'll deliver these timbers, but I don't think they're needed. If we don't have to season them, and if Ham is doing his part, I daresay we'll finish the ark in another moon."

"He'll do his part if that miner who's always coming about doesn't distract him from his work."

The next morning Ham was waiting downstream for the logs to arrive. He was eager to tell his father that the work would be finished in a week or two. He leaned against the ark as he sat waiting and endured the miner's disparaging remarks. "It's a box, not a ship," the miner told Ham, pointing to the blunt ends of the craft. "No stern nor bow—how can you ever steer the thing?"

"Designed for floating, not steering," Ham replied.

"You mean you'll commit yourself to a craft over which you have no control?" He laughed. "No need to think about it—with all the animals you're taking aboard, it'll sink in the harbor."

"Japheth tells me the stability of the craft will increase as it sinks lower in the water, that with a lower center of weight it'll be harder to capsize."

"So he says."

"When the waves strike the sloping sides they'll hit and roll rather than strike with direct impact. In that way the boat won't be broken in two."

"Or so you hope." He toyed with a leather bag. "You truly believe a flood is coming, don't you?"

"I do." He gestured toward the pouch. "What is it you have to show me?"

The long-nosed miner fished in his bag. Following the discovery of ore and the crude uses made of it, the invaders from Nod had developed a mining industry making molds, smelting, and casting. And now this, another discovery of some kind.

The miner carefully withdrew a handful of stones, and as he slowly opened his fingers Ham caught his breath. In the man's palm were several milky white stones, translucent with a pearly surface. "How would your wife like a string of these?" he tempted, a gleam in his eye. "We call them moon stones."

Ham tried to conceal his excitement. Of all the exotic things produced by Eastern people, none equaled the moon stones.

The miner poured the stones back in the bag, pulled the leather thong tight, and knotted it. *Now he will begin to boast*, Ham thought to himself, and he did. He boasted of having been far south and west to the Great Monument to the sun, a monument made of two and a half million limestone blocks, each weighing tons. Ham had heard the boast before and knew the miner would again disparage the step-sided ziggurat constructions people of the river valley built and extoll the genius of those who built the smooth-sided Great Monument.

The miner argued with Ham that the intelligence required to build such an edifice as the great pyramid was far beyond anything known in the East. "Yet," he said, "the people I met in that land, with their vast knowledge of the universe, have no faith in an invisible god such as you and your father worship."

"That knowledge you speak of—where does it come from?" Ham asked, and, not waiting for an answer, he explained, "My brother, Japheth, is the intelligent one of us. He understands the reckoning of time and space. He's explained to me the regularity of the heavenly bodies and the passage of days, months, and years—the reckoning of hours and minutes—all of it masterminded by God. That's why he thinks of the Creator as a mathematician."

"Mathematician? Hardly what I would want a god to be. You have another brother?"

"Yes. You would have little in common with him. His name is Shem. Not a practical man, I'd say, but gifted. Shem was quick to master the wooden pipes your people brought here, and he composes melodies never heard before. I'd say he seems content with beauty, and, like my father, he can be otherworldly, if you know what I mean."

The miner laughed. "Otherworldly? Anyone who preaches that water will cover the earth and drown everything is more than otherworldly; he's crazy."

Ham ignored the insult. "I once asked Shem what he thought of God, and he told me he thinks of God as an artist. Then he became ecstatic talking about the profusion of sounds and color everywhere in nature."

"And your father?"

"What does my father think of God? Hmmm . . . I'd say he thinks of God as savior . . . and judge. Yes, savior and judge. He believes God will judge humanity for sin and that God will save all who enter the ark. I believe the ark will float because God told my father how to build it."

"You're quite alone in that view."

"True, except for my mother and brothers. If you had lived all your life with a man like my father, you'd trust him, too."

The miner shrugged his shoulders. "And you," he asked, "What do you think of your god?"

Ham hesitated, then answered. "I think of him as provider. And, believe me, I expect to get what I want in this world. What you tell me about that monument intrigues me. In my head there is a vision—I dream of building a monument on the Shinar Plain that will be unequaled in all the world!"

"Ha! In all this plain there is no rock quarry—you have only packed clay and mud bricks for building." He laughed and, motioning toward the ark, said, "In the meantime, you waste your time on this monstrosity."

Ham controlled the impulse to punch the man and, speaking calmly, explained, "The work improves my skills for whatever I might do in the future. My job is to oversee the smelting of the pitch. The bitumen pits in the valley provide caulking such as a ship like this requires. It's flexible waterproofing that will yield to pressure without cracking, stretch without pulling away from the wood."

"Here comes your father."

Ham turned to see Noah, Japheth, and his great-grandfather, Methuselah, approaching.* The old man was speaking. "Where is Shem?"

"He's rounding up animals," Japheth answered. "Two of every unclean and seven of every clean."

The old man chuckled to annoy them. "Unclean? Clean?"

"Surely you know the animals we can eat and the ones we can't," Noah said.

"And the ones you can sacrifice and the ones you can't," Methuselah added. He eyed the sky, searching for signs of rain. "You say it will rain, Noah. How much rain will it take to flood the earth?"

Ham could see the weariness in his father's face as he struggled to convince Methuselah.

"That I do not know," Noah said. "It may do more than rain. God might shake the earth, cause the water of the gulf to rise—sweep over the land. However he chooses, God will put an end to all people, for the earth is filled with violence because of them."

"You've said that before," the old man argued, "and I'll tell you again: You're much too narrow for a man of your

---

* Scholars differ in interpreting the genealogies in Genesis 5. Some believe the spans of years given are those of dynasties, not individuals. If the numbers refer to lifespans, Methuselah was alive at the time of Noah and would have died in the year of the Flood. For my purposes I assume that the numbers refer to lifespans.

learning. God is a God of love who wouldn't destroy humanity made in his own image."

"He is holy," Noah argued, "and must punish sin."

"Sin! Sin! That's all you ever talk about." His thin voice was strident. "You blame the invaders for every evil in the world, but look at the skills and crafts they brought us. They're seafarers and shipbuilders, and they've opened up the world for us! If their warrior chieftains set their standards by the stars, who cares? I find them entertaining—refreshing, what with their sporting games and music, their dancing and races. You mustn't be so narrow, Noah. You're much too serious, too religious."

Seeing that Methuselah was too feeble to continue walking the length of the ship, Noah beckoned to Ham to bring the cart. The brothers rolled the old man to where the plans for the ark were sketched in clay.

Noah drew attention to the three decks as he again explained the construction to his grandfather. "Firm walls," he told him, "are braced by crossbeams going this way and that. See here." He pointed to the squares on either side. "These are rooms, cells that line the hallway running the length of the ark. Everyone aboard will live with the animals on the first floor. These ramps and stairs lead to the other decks where food, fodder, and water are stored."

"Live with the animals?" Methuselah chuckled. "How long do you think your wife will put up with all that dung, not to mention all the racket? Tell me, do you expect your sons to feed them all? Water them?"

"We've a plan for everything. We'll haul feed for the cattle from the lower deck in carts, up the ramps you see. I—"

"How long do you expect to stay on this ridiculous contraption?"

"It'll take a long time for the water to recede, so we'll be aboard for months."

"I've heard of people being aboard ship for months. Food

runs low; water becomes stale. People get sick and die."

"I understand that, so we're storing aboard ship the sweetest water in the land. It's water from ponds where cypress leechings make it pure. Seafarers swear by it, say such water never gets stale."

"I've heard the same. But with all those animals aboard, how will you get rid of waste?"

"Out the window."

"Hmph."

"Look up there—see the window? It runs the length of both sides. See how the roof overhangs? The window is well protected by the eaves. Plenty of fresh air. The support beams or ribs intersect the window at intervals and frame in sections of a cubit of space. Each section has a sliding panel that we can close when necessary. Wouldn't you like to go inside?"

The old man refused. Noah returned to the sketch and pointed. "In this room where birds will be kept, we've built a lattice over the window."

Ham interrupted. "Father, the men are ready to load the vats of water."

"Good. We'll start tomorrow."

The next day the crews began loading grain and water onto the ark. A message came from Shem that he was on his way home. Noah waited before the campfire and picked at the food set before him. Ham understood his anguish, for he knew how his father longed for relatives and friends to get on the ark, but Ham himself felt no anguish. *Either they believe or they don't,* he reasoned. *If they perish it's their own fault.*

Japheth commiserated with Noah. "My wife's sister is getting married soon. I tried to tell her there's no future outside the ark, but she won't listen to me. I thought if you and Mother spoke with her—"

"I will try, Son. If she listens, she'll be the first one."

Ham could not understand his father's persistence. In the

beginning when God first told Noah to prepare the ark and he relayed the message to others, they laughed at him, and if anyone seemed interested in what he had to say, then the jeering began. But as time wore on, people simply ignored him, sometimes with *polite* indifference.

Ham fell asleep quickly, but in the middle of the night he was awakened by shouts and curses. Throughout the rest of the night he heard loud threats and curses, a woman crying, and children screaming. It seemed to Ham that the strong were always shouting and the weak were always crying.

With the first light of day Ham heard the lowing of cattle, the barking of jackals announcing the arrival of Shem. He got up and went over to the ark to help. The gangplank was lowered, and the beasts were being corraled into makeshift pens. Suddenly Ham stopped dead in his tracks. Above the noise the Lord was speaking to Noah! "Go into the ark, you and your whole family, because I have found you righteous in this generation." Instructions about the animals followed, and then God said, "Seven days from now I will send rain on the earth for forty days and forty nights, and I will wipe from the face of the earth every living creature I have made."

The message threw Noah and his sons into a flurry of activity. Frantic to meet the deadline, the sons and their crews worked day and night. In the midst of it all, Noah was warning everyone within earshot that the Flood was coming within seven days. No one believed him, but the curious came to watch as workers secured the vats of water, the sacks of grain, and the animals in their cages.

On the seventh day Noah took his wife, their sons and daughters-in-law into the ark, dejected that no one else heeded his warning. As the workers gathered up their tools, they looked around one more time, awkward now that their long task was finished. "Sure you know what you're doing?" a shipwright asked, and Japheth nodded. "Positive."

"Won't you please change your mind and join us?" Noah pleaded. "There's plenty of room for all of you, your wives, and children."

The crew laughed in his face.

Noah, Ham, Shem, and Japheth, with their wives, followed the work crew to the door. Seeing the crowd at the foot of the gangplank, the workers took their leave without so much as a farewell. Over his shoulder, the shipwright yelled, "We'll be waiting when you come to your senses and give up on this."

The crowd hooted and howled obscenities.

Noah stood framed in the doorway, his family by his side, and weeping, he begged the people for the last time, "Friends, we have plenty of room, plenty of food and water—," but jeers drowned out his plea.

The women were weeping, too, bidding farewell to friends and relatives. Ham saw his great-grandfather sitting under a tree eating a melon, and he hoped Noah did not see him. Ham took hold of a cable that controlled the gangplank, ready to haul it up, when suddenly the cable was jerked from his hands as the gangplank was lifted in the air. Stunned, Ham watched as the heavy gangplank was heaved forward with an unhuman force and fell in place with a solid thud! Instinctively, he knew they were locked inside. Ham put his shoulder against the door to see if it would budge but shook his head. "God has shut us in."

Noah turned away, regretfully, and led the way into the family quarters where there was more light.

As strong as he was, Ham felt the nerves in his spine tingle as he tried to comfort his wife. The women were all weeping and trembling.

Noah, sharpening a stylus with a piece of pumice, sat down to write. The rubbery clay was pliable as he pressed the stylus against it. "Let's see, we brought seven sheep, seven cows . . ." and he proceeded to record the full inventory of cargo.

Still feeling the shock, the women managed to bring out food and set a meal before them. As Noah broke the bread and passed it around, his wife served butter and cheese, but no one felt like eating. Ham poured strong black tea, and his wife passed dried fruit and nuts.

"There's plenty besides," Noah's wife coaxed them. "There's plenty even if we stay aboard for some time." Trying to cheer them, she added, "I love the smell in here. Doesn't cypress smell delightful?"

No one responded.

Shem, his face grim, asked, "Father, if the water covers the earth, how will plant life be replenished?"

"God alone knows."

"If water covers the land," Shem persisted, "won't it take a long time for it to go down?"

"Yes, it will."

"Then what about the plants and flowers?"

Noah was thoughtful for a moment, then turned to Japheth. "Isn't it true, Japheth, that water in the high mountains freezes?"

"Aye, Father, that's true."

"And isn't it true that seeds and plants beneath ice can be preserved for a very long time?"

"I think so."

"Then perhaps that is the way God will replenish the earth."

A bowl of figs and pomegranates was being passed. Noah declined the food and watched the dust motes floating in the sunbeams streaming in from the window. "Listen everybody," he said, "I've started keeping a log of our voyage." Then Noah read aloud, "On the seventeenth day of the second month in my six-hundredth year, we entered the ark."

Suddenly darkness extinguished the sunbeams, and a rush of wind began battering the ark. Dashing to the window, Noah saw a roiling sky split with forked lightning. His heart pounding, he heard screaming as people outside ran panic-stricken. A dark column of cloud, twisting and turning, was weaving as it thundered toward them. As it passed over the ark, the noise was deafening.

Then, as if a great sheet holding water had burst, a deluge fell from the skies. The downpour rumbling on the roof sounded like thundering hoofbeats of stampeding cattle. Inside the ark birds were screeching, flying about in a frenzy, and the animals were in a wild uproar.

Rain lashed the ship for hours, then a deafening crack jolted the ark, and the earth groaned as if torn apart. Without warning a wall of water struck one side of the craft. When the wave rolled beyond, the ark was afloat!

As the storm continued day after day, there was no telling day from night. With the water rising, rushing, surging this way and that, pitching forward, then back, the ark bobbed like a cork in the turbulence but with amazing stability. Week in and week out, it rained and thundered, wind blowing, lightning flashing. But the snug craft proved its worth, and those aboard were able to perform the tasks of preparing meals and caring for the animals with few mishaps.

Noah's wife set up her loom and began teaching her daughters-in-law to weave. Noah and his sons found time to keep their tools in shape, and from time to time they talked. They speculated on the duration of the storm, and Noah could only tell them it would rain forty days.

"But there is more than rain," Japheth told them. "I believe there are earthquakes and tidal waves, that all the fountains of the deep are in revolt."

"That may be," Noah agreed, "for the abundance of water cannot come only from the skies."

During the night of the fortieth day, the wind stopped blowing, and they could hear the rumbling of thunder traveling further and further away. The sound of water pouring from the eaves stopped, and gently the patter of rain on the roof ceased.

The next morning when Noah's sons opened the window panels, the sun streamed in, and shouts of joy went up. But they also saw that the water was as rough as ever. Noah wrote in his log, "On this the twenty-seventh day of the third month, rain has ceased to fall."

But it was months before the water seemed at rest. When, for the first time since the storm began, there was calm, Noah wrote in the log, "One hundred and ten days have passed since the rain ceased, and only today has turbulence given way to calm."

Hardly had he written the words than he observed another wind blowing steadily. When it did not cease after several days, Japheth had a theory. "The wind is drying up the waters. God has sent the wind." The thought helped them endure the constant drone as wind moaned around the corners of the ark.

With the thought of the water assuaging, spirits revived. The women began singing as they went about their chores, and in the evening when the work was done, Shem played melodies on the reed pipe. The brothers found humor in their calamities and laughed as they had not for some time. But it was obvious that Noah's heart was heavy; he was thinking of those he loved who were dead.

To relieve the unsettling effect of the continual wind song, the women took turns telling stories. When the stories were exhausted, they began repeating them before going to sleep at night. Then, one night when they were sound asleep they were jolted awake by the ark bumping against something. A shudder went through the craft from one end to the other. Then the ark seemed to free itself, floated a bit, then struck something again, grinding, scraping as it moved.

Noah saw his sons, white-lipped, braced against the wall, holding their wives in their arms, too alarmed to speak. He smiled to reassure them. They would not be comforted, afraid the bottom of the ship was being ripped open.

The ark lurched, listed to one side, then righted itself. Ham found his voice and whispered coarsely, "We're coming on land."

Neither Ham, Shem, nor Japheth recovered from their shock until the ark remained solidly set for a while. Only then did they venture to move. They climbed up to the window and cautiously looked out. As far as the eye could see there was water, a smooth line against the horizon.

"I wonder where we are?" someone asked.

"I have no idea," Noah answered. "But we've landed, and that calls for a celebration."

That night, after celebrating the occasion with music and dancing, Noah wrote in the log, "On this seventeenth day of this seventh month the ark has come to rest. Water stationary."

The next few weeks were spent in frustration. There was no way of knowing how far the water was receding, and now that the ark was on land everyone was anxious to get out. Noah tried to keep their minds occupied by reciting history from the days of Creation, but they knew the history by heart and were bored. Speculation as to when they might be released was uppermost in their thoughts. "I know the water is receding," Japheth said. "We've been on land now for thirty-four days. If the water goes down at the rate of three cubits a day, it's gone down more than fifteen cubits."

Ham challenged him. "How do you know it goes down three cubits a day?"

"An arbitrary figure, Brother, an arbitrary figure."

"Then your calculations mean nothing."

But in the morning watch, Shem sighted the top of a

mountain. The others rushed to the windows and saw a faint blue outline of a hill against the sky. As their eyes grew accustomed to the view they began seeing another and another mountaintop.

Noah lost no time recording the sighting in the log: "On this first day of the tenth month the tops of mountains are visible. Ark on dry land. Water continues to settle. We wait but not with patience."

For forty days Noah and his family waited. Along with the regular duties of cleaning the stables, feeding the animals, and feeding themselves, the shearing of the sheep and watching over the birth of a calf helped pass the time. Even so, there were many long hours when all they did was gaze longingly out of the window and mark the infinitesimal lowering of the water level against the mountains.

Ham wondered what kind of a world awaited them once they left the ark, but he did not speak of it. The brothers talked about everything else but avoided that subject. Japheth spoke of ships and Shem of trees and animals and plants, until one day he spoke of birds. "Did you know," he asked them, "that shipmasters carry birds on long voyages?"

"No," answered Ham, "but why?"

"I don't know for sure. Perhaps for company."

"I know," Japheth said. "They take a raven or two in case they lose their way. If that happens, they have only to release a bird, and it'll fly in the direction of the nearest land."

He is, indeed, a clever man, Ham thought, as he considered what Japheth said.

The next day Noah followed Shem into the aviary and told him to fetch a bird. "The black one with the wedge-shaped tail." Shem threw a cloth over the raven and quickly grabbed it. Cautiously reaching beneath the cover, he held down the bird's wings, then removed the cloth. In the strong sunlight the black feathers shone glossy with a purplish sheen. The excited bird, its eyes angry, struggled as Shem stroked the shaggy throat feathers beneath its bill and spoke soothingly. Noah climbed up, opened the window and, taking the raven in both his hands, reached outside and let it go.

The raven flapped its wings rapidly, then sailed on its flat wings away from the ark. Noah watched until it disappeared from sight.

Throughout the day the family kept vigil waiting for the bird to return. "The raven is a scavenger, eats anything," Shem told them. "I daresay it will find plenty to eat, plenty of places to roost."

Later, Noah wrote in the log, "On the eleventh day of the eleventh month I sent out the raven. For seven days the raven has flown back and forth. Waters continue to settle. We remain steadfast."

The next day Noah asked Shem to get one of the doves from its cage. When the bird was brought to him, cooing and billing, *co-roo-coo, co-roo-coo,* Noah held it close to his chest, stroked the pale beige down, and carried it to the window. He lifted the bird outside the ark. For a moment it perched on his hand, its pink feet wrapped around his finger. Then the dove flew away.

Again the vigil, but this time, within an hour, Shem spotted the bird returning. "She's coming back!" he yelled and waited for the dove to light. "She hasn't the strength to circle—she's headed straight for the window ledge."

Noah was ready for her. He reached out and brought her inside. "Just as I thought. She could find no place to set her feet because there is water over all the surface of the earth."

Hopes sank, and the mood on the ark was one of gloom if not despair. "Cheer up," Noah told them, "in another seven days we'll try again. No doubt by then the situation will improve. Come along, Shem, can't you give us a little music?" But Shem declined.

That night Noah wrote in the log, "On this eighteenth day of the eleventh month I sent out a dove. The bird returned. Waters settle. We are weary but grateful to have survived."

After another week passed, Noah released the dove again. When it did not immediately return, feeble hope returned. As the hours went by, Noah's wife dared show some elation. But then, toward late afternoon, Ham spotted the dove making her way back to the ark. "Uh-oh," he said, and hopes were dashed again.

Noah stood by the window, ready to reach up and bring the bird inside. But she flew straight in, landed on the floor, and waddled about, a leafy twig in her bill. Excited, the family huddled around the dove.

"It's an olive leaf just grown!" Shem exclaimed and held it high. "Surely we won't have to wait much longer if the olive trees are greening again!"

"I say we'll be out of here within a week," Ham predicted.

The women, laughing, crying, ecstatic with joy, began dancing round and round.

"Well, Noah," his wife said, "you have something to write in the log today!"

"Indeed." And he wrote, "On this twenty-fifth day of this eleventh month, I sent out a dove. Within the day it returned, a newly grown olive leaf in its beak. Water must now be contained in rivers and streams."

And, within a few days, excitement was running at a fever pitch. Noah wrote another entry: "On this second day of this twelfth month, I sent out the dove again. She did not return. We are getting our belongings together, for surely we will soon leave the ark."

The waiting was not over. A week went by, then another, and another with no word from God. Ham eyed the door, studying it like an enemy, afraid of what lay beyond. "Father, there's no budging the door. Has God forgotten us?" he asked.

Noah did not answer. Instead, he beckoned Ham to follow as he climbed up to the window. Ham stood at his father's side as Noah took one more survey to decide if he might safely remove the covering of the ark. As he opened it, a gust of cold air struck them with force, and one glimpse of the devastation made Noah order the others to stay inside the family quarters.

At first glance the surface of the ground looked dry, but seeing great quagmires here and there, Noah shut the covering and told his anxious family, "We can't leave yet; there's too much mud, great areas of silt and debris. The animals would sink if we let them out. Be patient. Be patient. Surely, it can't be long now. God will tell us when it's safe."

And in his log he wrote, "On this first day of this first month of my six hundred and first year, I removed the covering, looked all around. No water can be seen, but the devastation is total."

After making the entry, Noah sat for some time staring into space. Ham, too, felt overwhelmed. What they had seen outside the ark was beyond imagination.

Another week went by. "Should I start another weaving?" his wife asked Noah, smoothing the cloth on her lap.

"Suit yourself," he answered, but in the days that followed she did not start another. The family was exhausted, worn out by the yearlong ordeal. "I think we should try to rest as much as we can," Noah told them. "Once we're out of the ark, we've a whole new life to begin."

Three more weeks passed until, on the twenty-seventh day of the second month when the earth was completely dry, God spoke to Noah, "Come out of the ark, you and your wife and your sons and their wives. Bring out every kind of living creature that is with you."

When Noah repeated the news to the family and they saw the door of the ark opening, pandemonium broke loose. Shem raced down the corridor, flung open the aviary and let the birds fly out in a wild flutter. Japheth stood in the open doorway, shocked by what he was seeing. Noah called to Ham, "Bring out the animals."

In a few minutes Ham reappeared, leading the little flock of sheep. The sheep came down the gangplank awkwardly, bleating as they came, and the sons of Noah corraled them within a rope. "Too bad we sheared them," Japheth said, his breath white in the frosty air. "It's cold out here." He went back for the goats.

The cold wind atop the mountain was strong, and there was ice about. Noah wrapped a cloak about his wife, who was trembling, not so much from the cold as from what her eyes beheld. The world was nothing like it had been. From the mountain peak they could see great cliffs where slopes had been slashed and carried away. Bare rock faces were exposed where once there had been forests, and the spindly beginnings of saplings were few and far between, precarious in the rubble. Animal bones were scattered about, ravaged by the Flood. In all the valley there was no sign of life, no smoke of fire, no dwelling of any kind, only a bleak landscape lying desolate. The birds they had let go were out of sight, the wild animals had scattered, seeking cover, and the eerie silence that hovered over them was chilling. Noah's wife leaned against her husband. "This must be the way Eve felt the day they left the Garden."

"We are not alone," he said. "Come, Dear, we'll build an altar."

Together with his sons Noah piled stone upon stone until the pile was waist high. "Now bring me some of the clean animals and clean birds," he told them.

There was no wood about, no fallen branch or brush. "Rip a board from the ark," he told his sons, "enough to roast the sacrifices." And while they did his bidding, Noah prepared a ram for sacrifice.

When the sons returned with the board, split and broken into lengths, Noah laid the pieces across the altar and sent

Ham's wife to the ark for coals from the fire. Noah laid the animal parts in order, lit the fire, and waited for the blaze to take hold of the fat. As soon as the meat sizzled in the flames, he raised his arms and led his family in praise to God.

Suddenly, as the succulent smell of the roasting meat was filling the air, the voice of the Lord God, sounding like roaring surf, was heard saying, "Never again will I curse the ground because of man, even though every inclination of his heart is evil from childhood. And never again will I destroy all living creatures, as I have done.

"As long as the earth endures,
   seedtime and harvest,
   cold and heat,
   summer and winter,
   day and night
   will never cease."

Then God blessed Noah and his sons, saying to them, "Be fruitful and increase in number and fill the earth."

Tears streamed down Noah's face and, in the bitter cold, froze on his beard as God continued speaking. "I now establish my covenant with you and with your descendants after you and with every living creature that was with you . . . Never again will all life be cut off by the waters of a flood; never again will there be a flood to destroy the earth. This is the sign of the covenant. I have set my rainbow in the clouds, and it will be the sign of the covenant between me and the earth. Whenever I bring clouds over the earth and the rainbow appears in the clouds, I will remember my covenant between me and you and all living creatures of every kind."

Trembling with emotion, Noah and his family gazed up at the heavens where a band of sapphire was spreading across the sky. The sapphire fused with rose and lavender—a perfect arc spanning the world from one horizon to the other.

STUDY QUESTIONS

1. If you had been alive before the flood, and were given only the circumstances of that day, would you have
   A. Helped build the ark?
   B. Sympathized with Noah as a man suffering from delusion?
   C. Tried to dissuade him and his family from their venture?

2. What was the motivation of Noah's faith?
   A. His desire to obey God at any cost.
   B. Fear of the consequences.
   C. Contempt for the evil of his day.

3. What parallels do you see between the circumstances of Noah's day and our own period of history?
   A. Little fear of God.
   B. Corruption, violence, evil imagination.
   C. Like Noah, there are those who find favor in the eyes of the Lord.

Something to Ponder: Since no one knows how long humans existed before the flood, are there clues in the Bible as to how far civilization had advanced? Could we expect a family of eight to be able to pass on all the technology of the past?

2

Job

THOUGH HE SLAY ME, YET WILL I HOPE IN HIM.

Scripture: Job 1–42

From the shadow of the city gate Satan listened to the elders conversing. From time to time he checked on these men to reassure himself that they were all in line. One of them, Eliphaz, was a gaunt man, an aesthete with suitable credentials for his age. Coming from the Edomite city of Teman, a town noted for the wisdom of its people, he was highly respected for his counsel. The high regard paid him had long ago made him self-assured, confident that he understood the ways of God and man. *He's definitely a man I can use,* Satan told himself.

Then Satan caught sight of the one man he loathed with a passion. As the tall, imposing figure approached the gate, men rose to pay him homage. Satan scoffed. *They honor him for his wealth and think his character impeccable. Stupid fools. Don't they know Job worships God only for what he gets out of him.*

Satan thought about the many years he had stood on the perimeter of Job's compound watching the patriarch going through his ritual of sacrifice—saw him rewarded with more and more land, foodstuffs, cattle, sheep, and servants. Yet never had the Enemy given Satan the opportunity to prove his point, to test Job's mettle. Always he was kept at bay as if Job, his family, and property were fenced in by an impenetrable wall. Given the chance, Satan was sure he could change Job, make him curse God and love evil rather than shun it.

Over the years the life of Job had caused many a man to turn to God, but Satan knew that he could reverse that trend if only the Enemy would allow him.

Enough of this, he said to himself. *The urgency of my work demands that I keep on the go.* Satan found many subjects easy prey, for they were not unfriendly to his causes. But Job was a challenge. During all his machinations, Satan had Job uppermost in his mind, and whatever worked with other people he remembered as a tool he might use if ever the opportunity came to have a go at Job.

As Satan raced about his business of beguiling souls, he angrily chafed under the restrictions laid upon him. Once the grandest of angels, Satan felt himself more worthy of acclaim than the One who occupied the throne of heaven, and since his eviction from that place he had thought of nothing else but revenge. It was galling that he was constantly humiliated by his Enemy—forced to ask permission for anything he wished to do. He longed to be autonomous, to act on his own without reference to the Sovereign One. But, alas, that day had not yet come.

Knowing he must soon assemble with all the other spirits before the Enemy, Satan tried to come up with some way he might obtain permission. In his mind he knew precisely what would break Job, and he lusted after that victory, knowing it would discredit the Enemy and champion his own designs.

As Satan approached the throne with his retinue he scorned Gabriel and Michael with their hosts praising and worshiping the Enemy. The throng of angels before the throne was, for the most part, obedient, willing to do whatever the Enemy bade. But Satan and his cohorts—lying spirits and spirits of divination who had rebelled with him that fateful day before the world was made—had only curses for the Enemy. He felt himself a prince among his peers and preened himself in the dazzling radiance of the throne, awaiting his opportunity to accuse Job.

One by one each angel was called to give an account and

receive instructions. At last came Satan's turn. "Where have you come from?" the Enemy asked.

Satan looked straight ahead unflinchingly. "From roaming through the earth and going back and forth in it." He posed calmly, serenely, if you please, never one to reveal his real purposes, and he pondered how he might accuse Job.

But the Enemy seemed to read his mind and asked, "Have you considered my servant Job? There is no one on earth like him; he is blameless and upright, a man who fears God and shuns evil."

Or so you think, the Devil muttered to himself. "Does Job fear God for nothing?" he replied, controlling the anger welling up inside him. "Have you not put a hedge around him and his household and everything he has? You have blessed the work of his hands so that his flocks and herds are spread throughout the land. But stretch out your hand and strike everything he has, and he will surely curse you to your face."

The Enemy's response was straightforward. "Very well then, everything he has is in your hands, but on the man himself do not lay a finger."

Satan could hardly contain his excitement, tempered though it was by the limitation set upon him. Confident that his scheme would work even though he could not harm Job physically, Satan flew into action. He had slick Sabean cattle thieves ready and waiting to pounce upon Job's oxen and donkeys, kill the hired hands, and make off with the beasts. He gave the signal, and they quickly swooped down on their prey.

Cackling with glee, Satan then put into play his cleverest device, the "fire of God" as humans called it. With a shower of lightning bolts he burned Job's sheep and shepherds alike until their charred corpses littered the pastures for vultures to devour.

Next he incited the Chaldean robbers lying in wait to attack Job's caravan. As soon as all the long train came into view, the Chaldeans swept down the dunes, killed the drivers, and confiscated both merchandise and camels.

Messengers raced to bring the dreadful news to Job, and Satan was ecstatic. "He's bankrupt! He's bankrupt!" he shouted. But he was not yet done with Job. There was one more blow to strike, the *pièce de résistance!* Ingeniously plotted, the plan was foolproof. *A wind storm sweeps out of the desert, destroys the house in which his children are. But I spare Job's wife. Ah yes, his wife will be a useful tool. She'll go to pieces, become bitter, torment him with her grief.*

And so it came to pass. With one shock right after another, Job received the terrifying news.

Satan watched expectantly as Job, surrounded by his servants, saw his hysterical wife being led away. He fully expected the man to shake his fist at the Enemy and renounce all faith in him. But no move was made. Satan was frantic. *Go ahead, man,* he screamed, *Curse God and die!*

But Job didn't. Instead, he raised his eyes to heaven and, gripping his cloak in both his hands, he ripped it apart, the sign of the pious when mourning. A servant handed him a razor and held the basin as he shaved off his beard and hair. Only profound grief called for such total abnegation. *Will he now renounce the Enemy?* Satan fretted, and to urge him on, he chanted, *Curse God and die! Curse God and die!*

Instead the man fell face forward on the ground. His voice cracking, he choked out the words,

> Naked I came from my mother's womb,
> and naked I will depart.
> The Lord gave and the Lord has taken away;
> may the name of the Lord be praised.

Satan cursed! *What a fool! The Enemy allowed this, should not Job at least charge him with wrongdoing?*

For days Satan fumed and fussed, pondering how he

might yet win. *What is left to do to him? I've done everything there is to do short of physical harm. If only—*

At the next assembly of angels and spirits, the tenacity of Satan served him well. As if flaunting his victory, the Enemy asked, "Have you considered my servant Job? There is no one on earth like him; he is blameless and upright, a man who fears God and shuns evil. And he still maintains his integrity, though you incited me against him to ruin him without any reason."

"Skin for skin!" Satan shot back. "A man will give all he has for his own life. But stretch out your hand and strike his flesh and bones, and he will surely curse you to your face."

The Enemy was swift to answer. "Very well, then, he is in your hands; but you must spare his life."

The bodily affliction Satan brought upon Job was as diabolical as he could conceive—boils from head to toe, a form of leprosy, an unimaginable agony. Satan laughed. *If Job could see what is back of all this pain it would strengthen his resolve. His ignorance is my advantage, for soon he'll blame his God for all his troubles. After that surely he will curse the Enemy.* And he leaned back to watch. In his reverie he recalled his great victory in Eden. *Even as Adam did not prove himself in opposition to me, so Job will fail.*

Satan did not concern himself with the purposes the Enemy had for letting humans suffer, but it bothered him that the Enemy's people were always the objects of the Enemy's love and never his wrath. From Satan's point of view they deserved wrath.

He dismissed the matter and, congratulating himself on his cleverness, reviewed the case before him. *There is Job sitting in the ash heap, his body covered with a painful skin disease, all his possessions, sons, and daughters are gone, and his wife is nagging him to "curse God and die."* Satan felt very smug. *How exceedingly clever of me to spare this woman to do my work, to persuade Job to do what I desire.*

From the ash heap Satan heard Job rebuking his wife.

"You are talking like a foolish woman. Shall we accept good from God and not trouble?"

Satan swore. *Of all the idiotic, naive, stupid* . . . again he flew into action—sent emissaries to fetch friends of Job whom he had handpicked for comforters. The four of them came trooping over the hill at sunset, their faces long and somber. So shocked were they by Job's appearance they withdrew a pace and sat down to wait seven days in silence to register their dismay.

Satan amused himself as he waited. Job's appearance, not to mention his odor, was enough to send a saint the other way. Eyes sunk back in his head, black circles under them, his mouth cracked and bleeding from fever, his feet swollen, running sores covering his body—Job looked less than human. Satan took pleasure in the humiliation Job felt, knowing it could lead to despair.

Bored with waiting, Satan livened things up by sending a terrible pain down Job's back. The sufferer sucked in his breath and held it, stifling a scream. Then Satan heard from Job's lips the first word of encouragement! "May the day of my birth perish, and the night it was said, 'A boy is born!' "

Eliphaz and the other three friends threw dust in the air, wailing as if Job had blasphemed. But he would not be quiet. "Why is light given to those in misery, and life to the bitter of soul, to those who long for death that does not come, who search for it more than for hidden treasure, who are filled with gladness and rejoice when they reach the grave?" He groaned his lament, pounding the earth with his fists and weeping.

Eliphaz rose to give answer; all eyes were on him. He was not unkind, but he scolded Job, reminding him that he had not talked this way when others were suffering and he was comforting them. "Think how you have instructed many, how you have strengthened feeble hands . . . But now trouble comes to you, and you are discouraged; it strikes you, and you are dismayed."

Satan urged him on, anxious that Eliphaz get to the heart of the matter.

The old man drew as close as he could to the foul-smelling Job, and the cord in his long neck swelled as he leaned forward and admonished him, "Consider now: Who, being innocent, has ever perished?"

That's it! That's it! Give him no comfort—moralize! Tell him he's self-righteous, fallen from the Enemy's grace, a godless man!

When Eliphaz seemed finished, Satan brought to his mind the dreams he had given him.

Wetting his lips, Eliphaz's rheumy old eyes widened, and he trembled for what he was about to say. "A word was secretly brought to me; my ears caught a whisper of it. Amid disquieting dreams in the night, when deep sleep falls on people, fear and trembling seized me and made all my bones shake. A spirit glided past my face, and the hair on my body stood on end.

"It stopped, but I could not tell what it was. A form stood before my eyes, and I heard a hushed voice: Can a mortal be more righteous than God? Can a man be more pure than his Maker? If God places no trust in his servants, if he charges his angels with error, how much more those who live in houses of clay?"

A whiff of the stench brought Eliphaz back to reality, and he moved away from Job. Flies were swarming about Eliphaz's mouth and nose, and as he swatted them, he called out to Job, "Call if you will, but who will answer you? To which of the holy ones will you turn?"

Job's wife, sitting before her loom, was weaving a woolen cloth, its pattern rich in color and design. Her narrow face, hard as flint, seethed with bitterness. How forcefully she threw the shuttle by which she shot the weft between the threads of the warp drawn up and down. The fire she had kindled was dying, so she stopped weaving long enough to lay more brush on it and to poke it vigorously. A shower of sparks shot up.

Eliphaz shook a bony finger at Job. "Man is born to trouble as the sparks fly upward," as much as to say, no one escapes trouble and trials. "But if it were I, I would appeal to God; I would lay my cause before him. He performs wonders that cannot be fathomed, miracles that cannot be counted."

That's good, Satan said to himself. *Get him to pray, to ask for a miracle. It'll do no harm. The heavens might as well be brass, for the Enemy won't intervene until this contest is over.*

Job drew up one knee and held it, grimacing with the pain, but he was listening. Eliphaz introduced another explanation for Job's suffering. "Blessed is the person whom God corrects; so do not despise the discipline of the Almighty. For he wounds, but he also binds up; he injures, but his hands also heal."

Good! Good! Satan agreed. *Get him to examine himself, scrutinize, analyze—become introspective, absorbed with himself. Let him grovel to no avail!*

Job did not take the bait but contended that he was innocent. Undaunted, Satan told Eliphaz, *Try the miracle proposal.*

Eliphaz obliged and told Job that God will automatically deliver the godly from every calamity of life. Job disagreed. He lifted his shirt, showed Eliphaz his back covered with maggot-infested sores and the blue wounds on his legs and arms. "God's terrors are marshaled against me," he said and begged for death. "Then I would still have this consolation—my joy in unrelenting pain—that I had not denied the words of the Holy One."

Satan scowled. *What a fool.* He sighed, weary with the tension. *At least he's blaming the Enemy for all this.* Of course, that was not the object. *Curse God, Job, and you'll know what an Enemy he can be!*

Job groaned. "My body is clothed with worms and scabs, my skin is broken and festering." Scraping his thigh with a piece of broken pottery, he scanned the faces before him but received no look of pity. It pleased Satan that the men were unrelenting.

Seeing his heartless wife busily working to pass the time while waiting out his fate, Job in desperation cried out to the Lord, "My days are swifter than a weaver's shuttle, and they come to an end without hope. Remember, O God, that my life is but a breath; my eyes will never see happiness again."

Seeing that his words moved no one, Job lay back on the mat and covered his eyes from the smoke of the fire and the whispers of his friends. They were discussing the next tactic, the next means of persuasion to their point of view. "Of course it's an incurable disease," Bildad said, "but he should not wish to die."

Take a man like Bildad, Satan said to himself. *As pious as they come but as shallow-brained as a flea—mouthing what someone else has said, never finding out for himself.* A Shuhite descendant of Abraham through Keturah, he was fond of pontificating. *I'd like to make Job a man like Bildad,* he thought.

The western sky was darkening, streaked with wine from the last light of the sinking sun. Somewhere a dove was cooing and there stirred a gentle breeze, wooing Job to give in to exhaustion. Satan crept up on Job and filled his mind with nightmares to anguish him throughout his fitful sleep.

As he tossed and turned, Job complained to God, "When I think my bed will comfort me and my couch will ease my complaint, even then you frighten me with dreams and terrify me with visions so that I prefer strangling and death. . . . Let me alone; my days have no meaning."

The success, though small, delighted Satan, and while he had the advantage he introduced another thought in Job's mind. *Consider how the Almighty seems intensely occupied with inflicting pain upon you,* and he made him wonder that God paid such attention to a man, examining him every morning, testing him every minute. *With such scrutiny, such infinite attention, surely he knows if you have erred.*

Job thought upon it, then spoke. "If it's a matter of sin," he said to God, "tell me what I've done."

Bildad bristled, repelled by Job's audacity; "All people sin!" Satan smiled at his lack of perception. Job did not claim the righteousness of the Deity, only the righteousness of a man living in right relationships with the Almighty and with other people. Job's integrity before others was intact; there was no blemish in his character, for if there was some imperfection, some unknown aberration, the Enemy would reveal it and, to Satan's chagrin, forgive it.

The condemning look on Bildad's face angered Job, and he railed out at God. "Why have you made me your target? Have I become a burden to you?"

Tell him he's a bag of wind, Satan told Bildad, and he did. Then he further antagonized Job. In speaking of the justice of God, Bildad told him, "When your children sinned against him, he gave them over to the penalty of their sin."

The words were salt in Job's wounds! He raged out at this cruel judgment on the fate of his beloved children. Had he not always entreated God for them? His children were not killed as punishment for their sin.

In the gathering dusk, only the evening star appeared, and Job's wife could no longer see to weave. Elihu helped her take down the loom.

Cajole him, Satan whispered.

"Surely," Bildad said, a bit more prudently, "God does not reject a blameless man or strengthen the hands of evildoers. He will yet fill your mouth with laughter and your lips with shouts of joy."

"Indeed, I know that this is true. But how can a mortal be righteous before God?"

The dark rim of a distant hill was cast against the evening sky, and above the brooding mountain, stars were appearing all across the heavens. Job's friends were searching the heavens for constellations. Job hobbled on his swollen feet to get a better view as he searched the northern sky for the Bear.

Finding it, he looked for Orion in the south. A cluster of seven large and many smaller stars, the Pleiades, hung in the eastern sky.

Job spoke aloud to no one in particular. "He alone stretches out the heavens and treads on the waves of the sea. He is the Maker of the Bear and Orion, the Pleiades and the constellations of the south. . . . Who can say to him, 'What are you doing?' "

Satan feared Job's conciliatory attitude and quickly tried to counteract it. *This should have been over long ago,* he fumed. *There he is wallowing in self-pity, thinking himself insignificant, hopelessly outmatched. Where's your pride, man? Curse God!* Then Satan remembered loneliness, and he caused it to consume Job.

His desolation so profound he could not weep, Job muttered as if to himself, "Although I am blameless. . . . It is all the same; that is why I say, 'He destroys both the blameless and the wicked.' "

His friends frowned and began to confer as Job continued muttering. "God is not a man like me that I might answer him, that we might confront each other in court. If only there were someone to arbitrate between us, to lay his hand upon us both, someone to remove God's rod from me, so that his terror would frighten me no more . . . I will say to God, Do not condemn me, but tell me what charges you have against me. Does it please you to oppress me, to spurn the work of your hands, while you smile on the schemes of the wicked?"

His friends were shocked at Job's audacity, but his wife, the hard flat planes of her face reflecting the firelight, sat with a sardonic smile on her thin lips. Satan perceived that she thought Job was about to break, ready to curse God and die. *She wants to hear him say it. Perhaps he will.*

Agonizing pain assaulting him, Job railed out at God, "If I hold my head high, you stalk me like a lion and again display your awesome power against me. You bring new witnesses against me and increase your anger toward me; your forces come against me wave upon wave. Why then did you bring me out of the womb? I wish I had died before any eye saw me."

Satan prompted Zophar to get ready to reply while Job changed his position, easing his left side where the dry flesh itched and tormented him.

Zophar stood to his feet, a commanding presence. He was a handsome man with a cherubic smile, using it now to soften the tone of his speech.

"If you devote your heart to God and stretch out your hands to him, if you put away the sin that is in your hand and allow no evil to dwell in your tent, then you will lift up your face without shame; you will stand firm and without fear."

Zophar continued talking at great length. Then standing across the fire from Job, Zophar leaned forward, arms outstretched, speaking earnestly, kindly, pleadingly, "You will surely forget your trouble, recalling it only as waters gone by. Life will be brighter than noonday, and darkness will become like morning."

Satan saw that Job was not impressed. He did not consider that he had anything to confess. He was searching the faces of each of them: Eliphaz with his thin shoulders bowed, his rheumy eyes staring back at him; Zophar, his pompous, rotund figure looking as if ready to belch from too full a stomach; and Bildad, his narrow face drawn down with lines, stonily waiting for Job to break. Elihu, the youngest of them, remained in the background, noncommittal, respectfully quiet in the company of older men.

Job's voice was as thin as a reed. "Doubtless you are the people, and wisdom will die with you! But I have a mind as well as you; I am not inferior to you. Who does not know all these things?"

Satan jabbed him with pain, making Job grit his teeth, yet he would not be quiet. "What you know, I also know; I am not inferior to you." He was breathing hard. "But I desire to speak to the Almighty and to argue my case with God. You, however, smear me with lies; you are worthless physicians, all of you! If only you would be altogether silent! For you, that would be wisdom."

Don't go, Satan told them, and they obeyed.

Zophar looked at Job patronizingly, as much as to say, "He feels bad. He wouldn't talk like this if he were not a sick man." Only Job's wife was disgusted with him; haughtily, she left the fireside and went inside the tent to sleep.

Job looked from one to another of the men and asked, "Would it turn out well if God examined you? Could you deceive him as you might deceive people?"

Bildad raised his hand to stop him, but Job waved him aside. "Keep silent and let me speak; then let come to me what may." Satan sensed that Job feared the risk of disputing with God and was afraid he may lose his life for doing so. "Why do I put myself in jeopardy and take my life in my hands? Though he slay me, yet will I hope in him."

Job's words stunned Satan because his entire strategy was based on the assumption that *a man will give all he has for his own life.*

Elihu handed Job a cruse of water from which he drank and then poured water on his head to cool his fevered brow. Satan could see that Job was growing weaker, struggling against the pain of his body and the misery of his soul. His voice was scarcely audible. "If only you would hide me in the grave," he told the Sovereign One, "and conceal me till your anger has passed! If only you would set me a time and then remember me!" The rasp of Job's shallow breathing sounded like a death rattle. Then he whimpered, "If a man dies, will he live again?"

Satan was encouraged by the question. It sounded as if Job doubted the Enemy's promise of resurrection. But before he could shout, "Bravo!" Job proved him mistaken. In his sick, tired voice, Job spoke to the Enemy about his own resurrection. "All the days of my hard service I will wait for my renewal to come. You will call, and I will answer you; you will long for the creature your hands have made."

Eliphaz interrupted him. Done with diplomacy he bore down on Job with a grueling inquisition that droned on and on. "Why has your heart carried you away . . . so that you vent your rage against God?" Job closed his hands over his ears, shutting out the endless argument.

When Eliphaz finished his lengthy diatribe, Job was ready with a reply. "I have heard many things like these; miserable comforters are you all! Will your long-winded speeches never end? What ails you that you keep on arguing?" And again he vented his spleen on God. "He seized me by the neck and crushed me. He has made me his target. . . . Again and again he bursts upon me; he rushes at me like a warrior."

Weeping, he put his face in his hands and sobbed.

Fool! Satan swore. *Curse God and die! Curse him! Curse him!*

But the stubborn man would not. When Job spoke again his weak voice was even, steady. "Even now my witness is in heaven; my advocate is on high." Satan was greatly agitated at the mention of the heavenly mediator. "My intercessor is my friend as my eyes pour out tears to God," Job said. "On behalf of a man he pleads with God as a man pleads for his friend."

Not that! Satan exclaimed. *He must not think of that intercessor!*

Job sighed heavily. "Have pity on me, my friends, have pity," he begged. "For the hand of God has struck me."

But the stony faces before him did not change. Looking away from them, he moaned in his misery, ready to die. "Oh, that my words were recorded, that they were written on a scroll, that they were inscribed with an iron tool on lead, or engraved in rock forever!"

Fat chance! Satan remarked.

"I know that my Redeemer lives," Job said, "and that in the end he will stand upon the earth. And after my skin has been destroyed, yet in my flesh I will see God." He thumped his thumb against his chest. "I myself will see him with my own eyes—I, and not another. I yearn for that day!"

Satan lashed out for another weapon, another device. *Guilt, guilt, that's what I need!* he shouted. Eliphaz came to his rescue, accusing Job of specific sins, his uncharitable spirit and actions, then entreated him to repent. "Submit to God and be at peace with him; in this way prosperity will come to you."

Job seemed not to hear and, in what sounded like delirium, yearned for the Enemy. "If only I knew where I might find him; if only I could go to his dwelling! I would state my case before him and fill my mouth with arguments. I would find out what he would answer me, and consider what he would say." He drew in his breath. "I don't know where he is," he confessed. "But he knows the way that I take; when he has tested me, I will come forth as gold."

A lopsided moon lay heavy in the eastern sky, slow to rise above the dark hill.

Satan saw that the comforters were failing miserably, so he let them sleep—first Bildad, then Eliphaz were nodding; only Zophar and Elihu were awake, and they half listened as Job recounted his virtues.

When Job stopped talking, a long silence followed.

Seeing that no one else was going to speak, Elihu slowly rose to his feet. His booming voice startled Bildad awake. Elihu, the Aramaean, was a volatile man, angry with Job because he justified himself rather than God and angry with the three friends because they had found no way to refute Job and yet had condemned him.

Eliphaz lit a torch that they might better see the angry young man. Dark with fury, Elihu's face was not yet fully bearded, the hair thin along his chin and cheeks. "I am young in years," he admitted, "and you are old; that is why I was fearful, not daring to tell you what I know. I thought, 'Age should speak; advanced years should teach wisdom.' But it is the spirit in a man, the breath of the Almighty, that gives him understanding."

Eyes flashing, he did not let up. "I gave you my full attention. But not one of you has proved Job wrong; none of you has answered his arguments.

"But now, Job, listen to my words; pay attention to everything I have to say. You have said in my hearing—I heard the very words—'I am pure and without sin; I am clean and free from guilt. Yet God has found fault with me; he considers me his enemy.' But I tell you, in this you are not right, for God is greater than humans. Why do you complain to him that he answers none of our words? For God does speak—now one way, now another—though we may not perceive it."

Then Elihu listed the various ways in which God speaks—through dreams, adversity, angels—and exhorted Job to listen or to say whatever he wished, for he wanted God to be vindicated. Job refrained, and Elihu continued. "Job says, 'I am innocent, but God denies me justice.' He says, 'It profits a man nothing when he tries to please God.'"

Elihu shook his head. "It is unthinkable that God would do wrong, that the Almighty would pervert justice.

"Oh, that Job might be punished for talking like a wicked man! To his sin he adds rebellion; scornfully he multiplies his words against God. Do you think this is just?" He faced Job, the hard line of his jaw rigid. "You say, 'I will be cleared by God.' Yet you ask him, 'What profit is it to me, and what do I gain by not sinning?'"

Elihu walked around the fire, threw back his shock of dark hair, his eyes black and foreboding.

Satan was greatly alarmed. *I did not tell him to say those things!*

Elihu turned to his audience. "So Job opens his mouth with empty talk; without knowledge he just keeps talking."

Then, concluding his speech, Elihu said, "The Almighty

is beyond our reach and exalted in power; he's too just and righteous to oppress. Therefore, men revere him, for he has regard for all the wise in heart."

Satan was infuriated by Elihu. *What right has he to speak for the Enemy!*

Job had no answer for the young man whose perception differed from his own. Satan's worry was that Job might realize that his adversity was one way in which God spoke to him. *That will never do!* Satan declared.

Daybreak was showing above the eastern horizon. Job's wife poked her head out of the tent, no doubt to see if Job was still alive, and, seeing that he was, withdrew again. Wind was blowing, the dust swirling, striking Job in the face.

Suddenly Satan was filled with great apprehension. He was not in control of the whirlwind. *It bodes no good,* he thought, and sensing the Personage approaching, he fled.

Job's friends huddled together, sheltering themselves as best they could. But Job, limp from illness and sheer exhaustion, made no effort to resist the storm. "May the Almighty answer me!" he said aloud.

And almighty God did answer him—answered him out of the whirlwind. "Who is this that darkens my counsel with words without knowledge? Brace yourself like a man; I will question you, and you shall answer me."

Job rose up on his knees, trembling at the thunderous sound of God's voice. A volley of questions bombarded him. "Where were you when I laid the earth's foundation? Tell me, if you understand." God surprised Job with questions that brought him face-to-face with the absurdity of his challenge.

There followed an account of Creation that caused all angels to shout for joy. God spoke of controlling sea waters within boundaries; the regularity of the planets in their orbits; the mystery of death, of light, of snow; the distribution of rain, ice, snow; the order of heavenly constellations; the control of the elements.

Job, humbled by the interrogation, held his breath, realizing he was in no position to question the One who alone created the world and governed it.

One question followed another as God described the providential care of wild animals; the curious habits of animal births; the freedom of wild donkeys and oxen; the silliness of the ostrich; the magnificence of the horse; the superb skills of the hawk.

And then the Lord asked, "Will the one who contends with the Almighty correct him? Let him who accuses God answer him!"

The controversy discomforted Job. God was answering Job's complaint to instruct and convince him. Convince him he did, for Job suddenly realized how awful it was to set oneself up a judge over God. Regarding God as his enemy was a grievous sin. How dare anyone to censure God!

Ashamed and contrite, Job answered, "I am unworthy—how can I reply to you? I put my hand over my mouth. I spoke once, but I have no answer—twice, but I will say no more."

The storm increased, whipping the tent flap, causing the men to lie on the ground, their faces covered.

"Brace yourself like a man," God said. "I will question you, and you shall answer me. Would you discredit my justice? Would you condemn me to justify yourself? Do you have an arm like God's, and can your voice thunder like his? Then arm yourself with glory and splendor, and clothe yourself in honor and majesty."

Job protested—the Lord was inviting him to ascend the throne of God, take over the reins of government and rule!

Job realized what he had done; in order not to give up his own sense of righteousness he had doubted the righteousness of God! The truth grieved him painfully. Sitting down in the ashes, he threw dust on his head and tried to answer God. "I know that you can do all things; no plan of yours can be thwarted. You asked, 'Who is this that obscures my counsel without knowledge?' Surely I spoke of things I did not understand, things too wonderful for me to know."

Tears streamed down Job's face, and his voice shook. "You said, 'Listen now, and I will speak.' My ears had heard of you, but now my eyes have seen you. Therefore, I despise myself and repent in dust and ashes."

Job knew his repentance would result in forgiveness of all that was sinful in his speeches. And there remained only the truth of his innocence and the truth of his holding fast to God, never cursing him during severe temptation.

Then God sought to right the wrongs done to Job. He addressed Eliphaz. "I am angry with you and your two friends, because you have not spoken of me what is right, as my servant Job has." Elihu was not guilty of misjudging God and Job. But God ordered the other three comforters to make a sacrifice of seven bulls and seven rams. The double sevens showed the profound seriousness of their sin, and they were told to go to Job and make reconciliation.

"My servant Job will pray for you," the Lord said, "and I will accept his prayer and not deal with you according to your folly. You have not spoken of me what is right, as my servant Job has."

When the Lord said nothing more, Bildad, Zophar, and Eliphaz rose up without a word to find the animals for sacrifice. Before the day was over, they returned leading the finest of their flocks. Slaughtering them before the Lord, they confessed their sins. Job prayed for each of them and then embraced them.

The reconciliation was complete. The contention between man and man, between man and God was over. The misery was over; Job felt health of body, mind, and spirit returning. But God had even more in store for him.

In the days that followed, Job's possessions increased until he owned twice as much as he had before. Then his brothers and sisters, and everyone who had abandoned him in his distress, eagerly returned. Effusive words of comfort about his past misfortunes were heaped upon him and congratulations abounded because his health and wealth were restored. People who would not come near him in his trouble feasted at Job's table. Each of them brought a gift of silver and gold and honored him once again.

In the years that followed, God gave Job seven sons and three daughters. There were times when he wondered if his offspring, like his sheep, camels, oxen, and donkeys, would be doubled in number, and when they were not, he realized why. *My seven children who died in the windstorm are not lost to me. I will see them again,* he told himself.

The beauty of the three daughters God gave Job was so great he chose names he thought appropriate. The first he named *Jemimah,* meaning "a dove," for her dove's eyes. The second, *Keziah,* meant "cassia," because she seemed as sweet as the scent of cinnamon. The third, the most beautiful of all, he named *Karen-Happuch* after the horn in which female cosmetics are kept. It was said that nowhere in all the land were there found women as beautiful as Job's daughters. To them Job gave inheritance along with their brothers.

Job lived to see four generations of his descendants. Through the centuries people have acknowledged his patience, for when he was sorely tried, he refused to "curse God and die." How valiantly he resisted the temptation when he was the focal point of a cosmic contest between God and Satan. Thus he vindicated the Almighty God and opposed the Accuser of humanity.

STUDY QUESTIONS

1. What does Job's experience teach you about Satan?
   A. That he is invisible, always actively engaged in accusing believers of God and tempting them.

B. That at times he controls well-meaning people.

C. That some of his acts are attributed to God.

2. How do you explain the faith of Job?

A. He understood the character of God.

B. Although he misjudged God, Job did not curse him because he trusted that his Redeemer would deliver him from the grave.

C. Although Job did not have a Bible there must have been an oral tradition of God's dealings with people that gave him faith.

3. If you had been one of Job's comforters, would you have

A. Suspected that sin caused such extraordinary suffering?

B. Guessed that all that happened to Job was the devil's work?

C. Acknowledge that you did not understand why it all happened but that you cared for Job and wanted to help him?

Something to Ponder: To rail out against God the way Job did seems to be the very antithesis of faith. How do you reconcile such railing with Job's strong expressions of faith in God?

3

Abraham

AGAINST ALL HOPE, ABRAHAM IN HOPE BELIEVED.

Scripture: Rom. 4:18; Heb. 11:8–19; Genesis 12–22

Sarai's handmaid had brought a basin and water to the tent, and Abram had washed himself. Tired from the day's work, he sank down on the mat to watch Sarai undo her hair. With the flap of the tent left open by the girl, he could see the last light of day fading over the trees.

This campsite close by Hebron was one of his favorites because the great trees of Mamre provided shelter as well as beauty. They reminded him of Shechem. And, although the city was in a shallow valley, it was on high ground, which made the air clearer and cooler than in the Dead Sea valley lying a few miles east. The Brook of Eshcol provided plenty of water, and the vineyards on the slopes provided the best of grapes and wine. This is, he thought, a lush and fertile land. In the twilight he could barely see the shapes of the tents occupied by some of his servants, and he started thinking about his sheep and servants ranging far and wide.

"Well, we've seen the world," she said, undoing the braids.

The curve of Sarai's chin and the white throat reminded Abram of a swan he once saw on the Euphrates when he was a boy. The swan glided in the water, and that was the way his wife moved, as if treading on air, her body yet slim and strong.

"That we have," he agreed. "Hmmm. Chaldea, Aram, Canaan, Egypt. . . . Did I ever tell you about when I was a boy and went to the temple of Nanna with my father?"

"The moon god? In Ur?"

"Yes."

Sarai laughed. "About a thousand times."

He grinned. "Oh, well, what's an old man for except memories?"

Sarai heaved a sigh, the last plait undone. "Yes, we're old," she said, the familiar sadness in her voice.

Beauty had never been enough for Sarai, nor would it be for any woman if she had a barren womb. Men from the East called a barren woman a coffin, and Abram thought the reproach must be the heaviest kind a woman could bear. Now that it ceased to be with Sarai after the manner of women, she grieved the more.

Abram tried to keep her mind off her grief. "As you were saying, we've seen the world. We know much about Chaldea. I lived in Ur long before you were born."

"Not so long. You were ten years old when I was born."

"I sometimes think of Ur, but I've never been homesick for the place."

"I remember a twenty-room house with water piped inside—beautiful couches, lots of servants."

"I enjoyed the library."

"A city does have advantages."

"Advantages over tent life, you were going to say. The advantage of a settled life as opposed to this being constantly on the move."

"That's right. But, then, I wouldn't want to live in Ur."

Abram chuckled. "You were only a spindly little girl running around barefooted when I first noticed you." It was his favorite story, and he enjoyed repeating it. "Your mother was sitting in the marketplace waiting for our father, and I saw you and your sister by the fountain. You were the prettiest girl I ever laid eyes on."

"You mean you never noticed me before that?"

"Of course, I knew you. But you were only one of many

little sisters until that day by the fountain I was struck by your looks."

"Half sisters," she added. "Even after we were married we didn't know each other well. Remember how it was?"

He nodded his head. "To think we lived in Ur all those years, and I hated every minute of it."

"Don't think you didn't let it be known!"

"There seemed no way out. Then my brother Haran died, and Father Terah didn't want to stay there after that. Never saw a man so grief stricken, have you? You'd think Haran was his only son." Abram was looking out over the encampment where the last of the campfires glowed feebly, sending up thin trails of smoke. "What an arduous journey that was up the Euphrates!"

"The barge was fun. Remember the barge?" She was brushing her long hair, bringing it down over her shoulder and separating the tangles.

"How could I forget. We were young and thought of it as an adventure, didn't we? But the rest of the way was anything but fun what with all our sheep and cattle. All along the way, seven hundred dreary miles, we looked for good grazing land, but we were months and months finding what we wanted."

"Then we came to the Balikh River, and, Abram, didn't Father think that an ideal location because the trade route from east to west passes there?"

"That's right. And, as you know, he named the settlement Haran after my brother who died in Ur."

"After your brother but not mine."

"Well, he was your half-brother the same as I."

The lamplight in back of her flickered, flecking her dark hair with gold. Abram felt privileged that he alone saw the long tresses falling loose about her shoulders. Once the tangles were straightened, the hair brushed, she would sleep. But in the morning, modesty required that she plait the hair in braids again.

"And when Father died," she continued, "you decided to pull up stakes and come here."

"Well, it wasn't my idea."

"I know. God told you to leave your country and kinfolk, which you did not do, husband. You brought our nephew Lot. God told you to go to a land that he would show you. So you did that, and we've been on the move ever since."

"That's true, and we may always live in tents, but God has promised us this land."

"And a family and descendants like the sand on the shore," she added.

Knowing the bitterness she felt, he went on quickly. "He's promised us more than all that. Today we live in tents; tomorrow or the next day or the next, we'll see the great city." She knew what he meant, and it always comforted her. He was quiet for a few minutes, then gently changed the subject. "You liked Damascus, didn't you?"

"Well, it was a city, but it was no better than Ur. When we left Damascus I was disappointed that we didn't travel the Bashan Road. They say the scenery is beautiful."

He shook his head. "A rough road, if you can call it a road. People tell me it follows wadis too steep and rough for easy travel. We'd never move all our flocks and herds and servants up and down those gorges. Besides, rugged country like that provides good hideouts for robbers, and there could be fortresses along that way."

She wasn't listening. "And beautiful trees, they say."

"True. The Phoenicians get their oars from those trees. But there were trees and the beautiful Mount Hermon range the way we came."

"And swamps."

"Well, yes, the runoff from the mountains makes it swampy in the Hula Valley, but the canal south of the lake takes care of most of the water."

"Is that where we crossed over?"

"Yes, at the ford. The road to Hazor wasn't bad."

"Nor was it good."

"Much better than the Bashan. We made good time getting to Megiddo."

"A walled city," she said, "and full of shrines."

"True. And it was there we had to make a choice, either west to Gaza or south to Shechem."

"For a man who didn't know where he was going, how were you led to go south?"

He didn't answer. "Ah, yes, south to Shechem. Shechem, so beautifully situated with Mount Gerizim in view—"

"Don't forget the idols."

"It was there, Sarai, at our encampment in that grove of the great trees of Moreh with their wide spreading limbs and welcome shade, that the Lord appeared to me and told me this is the land he will give our offspring."

"Our offspring, indeed!"

Ignoring her sarcasm, he continued to reminisce. "We built the altar, Eliezer and I, worshiped God, and moved on toward the hills east of Bethel."

"Everywhere you pitch our tent you build an altar."

"Isn't that as it should be? Besides, it declares our faith in the midst of heathen neighbors."

"We should have stayed at Bethel."

"We couldn't. There wasn't enough grass. You should know by now that a shepherd has to move where the grass is."

"But did it have to be the Negev?"

"That's where the water and grass were."

"When the drought came there wasn't enough of either. So, what did you do but take us all to Egypt."

"It was a temporary measure. Lot thought it was the logical thing to do since Egypt had grain."

"Perhaps if we'd never gone down to Egypt things would have been different with Lot."

"What do you mean?"

"I don't know what I mean exactly. It just seems that our going to Egypt was all wrong."

"Perhaps, but with the famine and all—I should've asked the Lord."

"Well, you didn't, and it's over and done with now. I must say it was hard to forgive you for having me lie like I did. I came within a hair of being taken by that wretched Pharaoh."

"The lie was the only way I could protect you, Sarai. You know the ruler's reputation: 'Pharaoh takes away the wives from their husbands whither he will, if desire seizes his heart.'"

"So we told them we were brother and sister."

"Egyptians respect a brother's rights. Theirs is a different system from ours—brothers are chief in families, not husbands or fathers; that's why the pharaohs adopt their wives as sisters."

"Even so, I barely escaped. And, you, what were you doing all the time I was being threatened? You were passing on the wisdom of Ur to the intellectuals of Egypt."

"Let's not talk about it."

Egypt was a sensitive issue for him, but there was something more he was worried about. Long after his wife fell asleep, he lay awake pondering what he must do. With Sarai past the age of childbearing, he knew he must find a way to provide the offspring God's promises required. Eliezer was his oldest home-born slave, born in Damascus, and according to the law, Eliezer would inherit whatever he had. As much as he loved his servant, he did not want that, and it bothered him greatly that he and Sarai were childless. Self-doubt plagued him.

Perhaps, he thought, *Sarai is right. Perhaps I'm too much a visionary. She's right about a lot of things, very practical. We've been in this land ten years. Was I all wrong in assuming we'd have children?* Then he corrected himself. *No, I was not assuming—God said I'd have offspring as numerous as dust. Why—*

Suddenly, out of the darkness, a vision came to him, and he heard God say, "Do not be afraid, Abram. I am your shield, your very great reward."

Abram rose up on his knees. "O Sovereign Lord, what can you give me since I remain childless and the one who will inherit my estate is Eliezer of Damascus? You have given me no children; so a servant in my household will be my heir."

"This man will not be your heir, but a son coming from your own body will be your heir."

Then God took Abram outside the tent. Millions of stars spangled the sky and frost lying about on the ground sparkled. God spoke again. "Look up at the heavens and count the stars—if indeed you can count them." Then God said to him, "So shall your offspring be."

Abram believed God would do what he said he would do, and the burden rolled off him. All his doubts vanished, and his heart was filled with joy.

The next morning, Abram told Sarai of his vision, and before the day was over, she had a plan. Her reasoning was simple; unable to bear a child herself, they would do the next best thing. According to Canaanite custom, a wife could give her maid to her husband and, if a child was born, claim it as her husband's heir.

When Abram returned to the tent to go to bed Sarai was waiting for him. "The Lord has kept me from having children. Go, sleep with my maidservant; perhaps I can build a family through her."

The pain in her eyes told him how deeply she sorrowed that this was the way it must be. He took her in his arms and comforted her. "She's waiting," she whispered and turned her face away thinking he'd not see her tears.

"Which one?" he whispered hoarsely.

"Hagar, the girl we got in Egypt."

In the course of time, a son was born to Hagar, and Abram claimed him as his own, naming him Ishmael. During the years that followed, Abram grew fond of the boy, played with him, taught him what he knew. Ishmael was thirteen, Abram, ninety-nine, when the Lord appeared to Abram again and said, "I am God almighty, walk before me and be blameless. I will confirm my covenant between me and you and will greatly increase your numbers."

Abram fell on his face before the Lord, and God said, "As for me, this is my covenant with you: You will be the father of many nations. No longer will you be called Abram: your name will be Abraham, for I have made you a father of many nations.* I will make you very fruitful; I will make nations of you, and kings will come from you. I will establish my covenant as an everlasting covenant between me and you and your descendants after you for the generations to come, to be your God and the God of your descendants after you. The whole land of Canaan, where you are now an alien, I will give as an everlasting possession to you and your descendants after you, and I will be their God."

Then God told him, "You are to undergo circumcision, and it will be the sign of the covenant between me and you. For the generations to come, every male among you who is eight days old must be circumcised, including those born in your household or bought with money from a foreigner— those who are not your offspring."

After that God spoke of Abraham's wife. "As for Sarai your wife, you are no longer to call her Sarai; her name will be Sarah.† I will bless her and will surely give you a son by her. I will bless her so that she will be the mother of nations; kings of peoples will come from her."

Abraham laughed and thought to himself, *Will a son be born to a man a hundred years old? Will Sarah bear a child at*

---

* *Abram* means "exalted father"; *Abraham* means "father of many."
† *Sarah* means "princess."

the age of ninety? And he pled with God, "If only Ishmael might live under your blessing!"

"Yes, but your wife Sarah will bear you a son, and you will call him Isaac. I will establish my covenant with him as an everlasting covenant for his descendants after him. And as for Ishmael, I have heard you: I will surely bless him. . . . He will be the father of twelve rulers, and I will make him into a great nation. But my covenant I will establish with Isaac, whom Sarah will bear to you by this time next year."

Then God went up from him. Abraham obeyed God, having himself, Ishmael, and every male in his retinue circumcised.

Not long afterward, while he was resting at the entrance to his tent, Abraham looked up and saw three men standing nearby, such men as he had never seen before. His heart beat rapidly as he bowed to the ground before them. Raising himself, he moved a few feet, then bowed again. Ten times he bowed as he approached them. Then he entreated the three to visit with him. "Let me get you something to eat, so you can be refreshed and then go on your way—now that you have come to your servant."

When they consented, Abraham hurried back to the tent and told Sarah to prepare dough and make bread while he fetched a calf for the meal. Sarah immediately recognized the honor of this occasion and, not trusting the cooking to a servant, began sifting the finest wheat flour to make unleavened bread. Abraham personally attended to the slaughtering of the fatted calf.

While the bread was baking on the hot stones about the fire, Abraham skewered small pieces of veal on spits and placed them over the fire to cook rapidly. While the meat roasted, he prepared the curdled milk. When all was done, he brought the meal outside to be eaten under the trees.

"Where is your wife, Sarah?" the men asked.

Abraham pointed to the partition separating the women's part of the tent from the men's. "Inside."

The men began eating, obviously enjoying the food. After they were finished, one of them told Abraham, "I will surely return to you about this time next year, and Sarah your wife will have a son."

The news startled Abraham, and he didn't know what to say. He knew Sarah was listening behind the partition, and he suspected she would laugh at such a statement.

One of the visitors asked, "Why did Sarah laugh and say, 'Will I really have a child, now that I am old?'" And Abraham realized the one speaking was the Lord. "Is anything too hard for the Lord?" the visitor asked. "I will return to you at the appointed time next year, and Sarah will have a son."

Sarah, from behind the curtain, answered. "I did not laugh."

But the Lord said, "Yes, you did laugh," for she laughed in her heart and the Lord knew it.

The Lord was gracious to Sarah; as he said he would do, he did. She became pregnant in her ninetieth year and bore a son at the time God had promised. Abraham named him Isaac, and when he was eight days old, Abraham circumcised him.

Abraham was handing his son to Sarah, carefully placing him in her arms for nursing. "We were as good as dead, weren't we," he said, "and look what God has given us!"

Sarah looked up at him, her eyes shining, "God has brought me laughter, and everyone who hears about this will laugh with me. Who would have said to Abraham that Sarah would nurse children?"

What followed was not easy for Abraham. Torn between affection for both his sons, he was aware of Ishmael's growing jealousy. The boy was growing into manhood and asserting his rights as the firstborn, lauding it over the baby. His attitude did not improve over the next months and years until, finally, when a great feast was given to celebrate Isaac's weaning, Ishmael showed contempt.

Sarah called Abraham aside. "I saw him mocking—making fun of me and the child. Something about my being so old—I didn't hear quite what he said. Just like his mother, contemptible!"

Abraham tried to wave her aside. She grabbed his sleeve. "Get rid of that slave woman and her son, for that slave woman's son will never share in the inheritance with my son Isaac."

Abraham turned away and went outside, greatly distressed. How could he send Ishmael away—he loved the boy—he was his own flesh and blood. If he lifted his eyes he knew he could see him now—standing by the tree, a handsome stripling, ready to take on the world. He thought of the good times they'd had together. And he thought of Hagar. *Poor woman, she's done nothing to deserve this.*

God answered his dilemma. "Do not be so distressed about the boy and your maidservant. Listen to whatever Sarah tells you, because it is through Isaac that your offspring will be reckoned. I will make the son of the maidservant into a nation also, because he is your offspring."

Abraham didn't sleep that night. Because of his tumbling and tossing, Sarah couldn't sleep either, so she finally got up and lit the lamp. "It's something you must do," she told him. "If Ishmael remains in your household, he can claim the inheritance. The only way you can make clear your intention is to publicly disown him, send him away."

"I know that, Sarah," he said wearily. "It's just that it's so hard." He put his face in his hands, trying not to weep, and she put her arms around him.

Early the next morning Abraham gathered together some food and a skin of water and went to Hagar's tent. He tried to tell her that this was what God told him to do, but he couldn't make her fully understand. Embracing the boy, he told them good-bye and watched as they went down the road leading south. *How will she ever make it to Egypt,* he wondered. His heart breaking, Abraham stood looking after them until they were out of sight.

Slowly he made his way back toward Sarah, who was standing in the tent door, Isaac in her arms. His head bowed for the heaviness of his heart, Abraham did not see her let the child down, but when he opened his eyes the boy was toddling toward him. *She knows what will cheer me,* he thought, and stooped down so Isaac could run into his arms. Lifting him up on his shoulder, Abraham felt the boy's chubby arms around his neck squeezing, rubbing his head in his father's beard. Abraham kissed his soft cheek, tickled him under the chin, making Isaac squeal with delight.

Sarah came outside. Seeing her, the boy started wiggling to get down; Abraham obliged. Sarah took one of Isaac's hands and Abraham the other and swung the boy along. A puppy came romping toward them, and Isaac pulled free of his parents to go after the dog. Gazing adoringly after him, Sarah said, "To think, God has promised to bless all the families of the earth through us, through this child, this bone of our bone and flesh of our flesh. Do you think we will live to see that day?"

"Perhaps. The hope of it gives me strength at times like this."

Sarah took his arm, leaned her head on his shoulder. "You did the right thing."

Roaming wherever the needs of the flocks led them, Abraham and his family came to Beersheba, where Abraham's servants had dug a well. For some time they stayed in that region of the Philistines, and while they were there, Abraham taught his son everything he knew about God. He told him the Lord is a personal God, not like the gods his forefathers served. "God is faithful," he told him. "His wisdom is infinite; his goodness will follow us all the days of our lives. The almighty God created all that you see, and as witness of that we rest as he did on the seventh day. God possesses heaven and earth and controls the forces of nature. He is the sovereign judge who destroyed the earth with a flood and will judge every person."

On many occasions Abraham recited to Isaac the history of humankind. And he explained the meaning of sacrifice. "Humanity's sin causes death. That's why we make sacrifices—the innocent lamb's blood is shed for us who have sinned."

Foremost in Abraham's mind was the importance of the covenant. "I exalt the Lord for he speaks to people—sometimes in dreams, sometimes by an angel, by visions, and by the spoken word. He has spoken to me, your father, Abraham." And then he repeated the promises God made to him. "God said he will make a great nation of us, of our people. He said the name of Abraham will be great in the earth. He promised that anyone who blesses us will be blessed and that anyone who curses us will be cursed."

The boy's eyes always widened and shined like his mother's when Abraham came to the last part of the covenant. "Through you, Isaac, and your descendants, God will bless all the families of the earth."

"How, Father, how?" he asked.

"I cannot tell you, Son. But as humankind was cursed by the sin of Adam, humankind will be blessed through a seed borne in our family. Isaac, that prospect will make anything you must endure worthwhile."

Abraham enjoyed the long, lazy days spent with his son in the environs of Beersheba. One day he took Isaac to see the well his men had dug and explained the construction. The boy was an eager learner, and that evening, as Isaac was explaining the well to his mother, Abraham went into the tent to rest. Hardly had he laid himself down when he heard the voice of God. "Take your son, your only son Isaac, whom you love, and go to the region of Moriah. Sacrifice him there as a burnt offering on one of the mountains I will tell you about."

The command came as a shock, and it was some time before Abraham recovered his wits enough to think upon the matter. As he waited for the courage he needed, words God had spoken years before sounded over and over in his head, "My covenant I will establish with Isaac . . . my covenant I will establish with Isaac." A growing conviction steadied him as he reasoned, *If Isaac is to inherit the promises made to me, he must live, or if he dies, God must raise him up, for it is impossible for God to lie, to go back on his promises.*

After a while, he was able to roll over and go to sleep. Early the next morning before anyone was about, Abraham was up saddling his donkey. As he tossed the blanket over the animal's back, his son came out of the tent, rubbing his eyes sleepily. "Fetch me two servants," he told the boy.

As Isaac obeyed, Abraham cut wood and debated whether or not to tell Sarah what his mission was. Finally he concluded, *this is a private matter between myself and God.* He felt he could not tell the boy lest he cause him untold anxiety. And if he could not tell the boy, how could he tell his mother? When the men came, he had them load the wood on the donkey.

By the time they were ready to leave, Sarah was up and asked him where they were going.

"To Mount Moriah to worship God."

"*Mount Moriah?* When will you be back?"

"Six days, give or take a bit."

Looking worried she came closer to say good-bye. "God wills it," he told her. And she said, "Very well, then."

As they set out on the journey, the servants leading the

pack animal and Isaac walking alongside, Abraham was satisfied that Sarah would not worry. During their long years together she had grown to trust God no matter what he told Abraham to do.

The road was dusty, and the day was windy as they walked north. Abraham wondered why God was sending them so far. *Why not let us go to one of the nearby hills,* he thought. The boy was walking ahead of him now, impatient to get where they were going. *He's beginning to look like Ishmael,* he told himself. *I'd say he's nearly the age of Ishmael when I sent away the boy and his mother.*

The little party camped in a cave the first night, which sheltered them from the wind, but there were bats and creeping things inside the cave that annoyed them. The second day they began the uphill climb, a slow, steady grade that soon brought the Moriah range in sight. By nightfall the wind had died down, and they chose a campsite by a brook.

After the boy was asleep, Abraham tucked him in against the chill of the night. Worn out by two days' travel, Isaac slept soundly, and Abraham watched him as he slept, breathing in, breathing out, slumbering in the strong rhythm only the innocent know. *Tomorrow I must tell him,* Abraham thought. *He's strong. He could get away from me, run down the mountain.*

On the morning of the third day, Abraham sighted the designated mountain in the distance. After breakfast he told the servants to unload the wood from the donkey, and then with his own hands he transferred the wood to his son. Scooping up coals from the fire, Abraham dumped them in an earthen jar that he would carry by one of the handles. He felt about his sash, making sure the knife was there, then told the men, "Stay here with the donkey while I and the boy go over there. We will worship, and then we will come back to you."

They had scarcely begun the climb when Isaac asked, "Father?"

"Yes, my son?"

"The fire and wood are here, but where is the lamb for the burnt offering?"

An answer came to him. "God himself will provide the lamb for the burnt offering, my son." And the two of them continued up the mountain.

Isaac was an observant boy, interested in everything nature offered. Along the trail he discovered hoofprints of the wild goats that foraged on the craggy slopes and drew attention to the wildflowers sprouting from the rocks.

By midmorning they were not far from Salem, the city of Melchizedec, but the Jebusites living there often attacked strangers, so they skirted the town. Just outside Salem they reached the place where he thought God had told him to make the sacrifice. He stopped, put down the jar of coals. "This is where we'll build the altar," he said. While Abraham was catching his breath from the long climb, Isaac put the wood down and began gathering stones.

Abraham looked down on the Valley of Hinnom in the west where it curved from south to east. The Hinnom was joined by the Kidron Valley whose river flowed between Mount Moriah and the hill of olives beyond. *Yes, this is the right place,* he said to himself and began laying stones one upon another.

As he worked, perspiration wet his brow and soaked through his cloak, but the mountain breeze cooled him. Isaac was struggling to bring a large rock, and Abraham allowed him to struggle, knowing the boy's independence. When they put that stone in place, the altar was finished. Isaac was breathing hard, and Abraham let him rest.

In a little while, the boy was ready to go on with the sacrifice and stood up to help. Abraham removed the thongs that bound the wood, placed the wood on the altar, then faced his son. Holding the thongs in his two hands, Abraham saw the realization dawn on the boy. *He can run,* Abraham thought, but knowing his son, he didn't think he would. Isaac trusted him and believed what Abraham believed about God.

He waited until the boy reached out his hands for his father to tie them. Like any other sacrifice he must be secured: Once he was bound, Abraham helped him onto the altar.

Abraham's knees felt weak. As he reached for the knife, he stared at his son's face, the dark eyes closed so as not to see. Raising the knife at arm's length, Abraham lifted his eyes to heaven and was ready to slay his son with one thrust when God cried out, "Abraham! Abraham!"

"Here I am," he answered.

"Do not lay a hand on the boy. Do not do anything to him. Now I know that you fear God, because you have not withheld from me your son, your only son."

The sense of relief left Abraham weak as water. Tears sprang from his eyes as he cut the thongs binding his son.

Isaac opened his eyes, looked about, asking, "What's that?"

Then Abraham heard it—the bleating of a sheep or goat, and looking around he saw a big buck of a ram with its horns entangled in a thicket. Isaac jumped down from the altar, and the two of them hurried to retrieve the ram. Isaac held the ram while Abraham wielded the knife, then together they dragged it up to the altar.

As the smoke from the burnt offering was swept away by the wind, Abraham told Isaac he would name that place "The-Lord-Will-Provide."

And for two thousand years afterward it was said, "On the mountain of the Lord, it will be provided."

STUDY QUESTIONS

1. What does Abraham's experience teach you about living in an alien culture?
   A. That there are moral tensions and dilemmas living in a carnal environment and that compromise leads to ruin.

    B. Abraham did not complain about the heathen among whom he lived.

    C. Abraham's habit of building an altar wherever he pitched his tent was a witness to heathen neighbors; an example that a believer today can follow by personal and public worship.

2. Faced with the fact of Sarah's barren womb and God's promise of children, would you

    A. Have waited for God to work a miracle?

    B. Have resorted to adoption?

    C. Have given up hope?

3. In what way might a parent be asked to put a child on the altar for God?

    A. Before the child is born.

    B. When the child is critically ill.

    C. When the child wants to serve the Lord in a dangerous place.

Something to Ponder: Mount Moriah is that range of mountains where Jerusalem is built. Not only did the Lord provide the ram caught in the thicket, he provided the Lamb of God who was crucified on that same mountain.

4

Joseph

YOU INTENDED TO HARM ME, BUT GOD INTENDED IT FOR
GOOD.

Scripture: Ps. 105:17, 18; Heb. 11:22;
Genesis 37, 39–50

J oseph could scarcely remember what his mother, Rachel,
looked like. But the burial was vivid in his memory—his
father, Jacob, holding the newborn baby in his arms; Jacob's
other wives and their children standing with the servants,
weeping.

As often as he could, Joseph went to Ramah and visited
Rachel's tomb and tried to remember his childhood in Haran.
His father was fond of telling the story of how he worked to
marry Rachel and how long they waited for a son. "Then,
when I was ninety years old, my dearly beloved Rachel finally gave birth to you, my dearly beloved Joseph, son of my
old age."

About the long journey back to Canaan, Joseph remembered only the crossing of the Jabbok River and the fear he
felt. Esau, his father's brother, was coming to meet them with
four hundred armed men. Joseph's father did not come home
that night. The next morning Jacob came home limping and
told the family that his name was now Israel. At the time no
one explained to Joseph why his father's name was changed.
Ever after that night, Jacob walked with a limp.

Of his father's twelve sons, Benjamin was Joseph's only
full-fledged brother, the rest of them having been born to his
father's other wife and concubines. The other wife, Leah, was

his mother's sister, and the two concubines had been the sisters' handmaids, Zilpah and Bilhah. Growing up, Joseph enjoyed his little brother and was more attached to Benjamin than to the others.

The older brothers were jealous of Joseph. Being the son of his father's favorite wife and son of his old age made Joseph his father's favorite. In addition, Joseph was different from the older sons; they could be cruel. Joseph's brothers massacred the men of Shechem. The shameful crime was brought on because Dinah, Leah's daughter, was violated by Shechem, son of the ruler. When Shechem wanted to marry her, the brothers sought revenge. "Before you can marry Dinah," they said, "all the males of Shechem must be circumcised."

The men of Shechem complied and were circumcised. While they were in pain, Simeon and Levi attacked and killed every male living there.

Jacob was incensed, but the deed was done.

After the incident, Joseph's father turned even more to the son he adored. He made Joseph the chief shepherd over the sons of Bilhah and Zilpah. The brothers resented Joseph and would not cooperate, so he reported them to their father.

Jacob flew into a rage, punished the brothers with extra duties, and sought for a way to reward Joseph. In a few days a peddler came to Mamre bearing wares he had bought from a caravan passing through Dothan. Among his offerings was a beautifully ornamented robe, which Jacob fancied. It was a tunic fashioned for a man of leisure—long sleeves, ankle length, woven with red and gold threads. Jacob bought it for Joseph.

After that Joseph did not go out to tend the sheep but wore the ornamental robe as a man of distinction. The promotion angered his brothers so much they would not give him the customary greeting, "Peace be to thee." The salutation was a sacred duty, and to withhold it was a sign of hostility.

Jacob, unaware of the way his sons treated Joseph, was

nevertheless made aware of their other sins. His concubine Bilhah was young for the elderly Jacob, and Reuben, his firstborn son, lay with her. For such a sin the outraged father would surely disinherit Reuben and give the birthright to another son. The brothers knew Joseph would be his choice.

Jacob and his family were living at Mamre in the valley of Hebron where Abraham had camped so many years before. A small field of barley was cultivated there, and all Jacob's sons except Joseph were reaping it, binding the barley into bundles, and stacking the sheaves in the field. During the heat of the day everyone stretched out under the shade of the giant trees to sleep.

It was after that nap that Joseph woke up and excitedly began telling them, "Listen to this dream I had! We were binding sheaves of grain out in the field when suddenly my sheaf rose and stood upright, while your sheaves gathered around mine and bowed down to it."

Dead silence greeted him. Finally Reuben spoke. "So? Do you intend to reign over us? Will you actually rule us?"

Joseph saw their countenances were hard and unyielding, but he was too excited to care. The next morning he had another dream to tell them. "This time the sun and moon and the eleven stars were bowing down to me."

Jacob frowned. "What is this dream you had? Will your mother and I and your brothers actually come and bow down to the ground before you?"

Joseph acknowledged what seemed obvious. His brothers' hatred worsened.

When grass near the Hebron campsite had been thoroughly grazed, Judah said, "We'll go to Shechem. There's an abundance of water there, plenty of grass."

Levi looked dubious. *He's remembering the massacre,* Joseph thought.

"Fear not, dear brother," Simeon said, "the terror of the Lord is upon all our enemies there."

"Shechem is three days' journey," Asher complained. "It's almost sixty miles. With the flocks and dogs—"

But Judah was dead set on going. Soon, with the sheep trotting behind them, they were heading north. Looking after them, Joseph doubted that they would feel any remorse revisiting Shechem.

Weeks went by, and when the brothers did not return, Jacob became concerned and sent Joseph to see if all was well.

Joseph, bearing cheese and bread for his brothers, made the trip in three days, but his brothers were not in Shechem. Wandering onto the Plain of Esdraelon, he did not know what to think. A field hand looked up from his reaping. "What are you looking for?"

"I'm looking for my brothers," Joseph answered. "The sons of Jacob. Have you seen them grazing their flocks?"

The grizzled man wiped his brow. "They've moved on from here. I heard them say, 'Let's go to Dothan.' "

"How far is that?"

"Twenty miles, give or take a mile or two."

I'll never make it before nightfall, he thought, and started the long trek.

Joseph was eager to see Dothan, for it was situated where the caravan routes from Asia Minor and Mesopotamia met. Travelers refreshed themselves at the wells and cisterns there. But as night came on, Joseph was still a distance from Dothan. He took shelter under a boulder, ate of the cheese and bread, watched the stars come out, then lay down to sleep.

By afternoon of the next day, Joseph came into the Valley of Dothan. Stretching before him lay lush pastureland and flocks of sheep. *Perhaps they're my brothers' sheep,* he thought and hurried to find out.

Coming in sight of the shepherds, Joseph hollered, "Hallo!" Then he recognized Judah and started running toward him. As he ran across the field waving, shouting, "Judah! Reuben! Asher!" they did not answer but moved closer together. As he drew nearer, one of them laughed. "Here comes that dreamer!" Then they rushed upon him and threw him to the ground. He yelled, "Brothers! Stop! What are you doing!" They were stripping away his robe as he struggled.

The robe torn from Joseph's body, they dragged him to a cistern and shoved him into it.

Joseph lay dazed. In the pear-shaped stone enclosure a narrow shaft of light streamed down from the mouth. Struggling to his feet, he was glad there was no water in the cistern. Feeling the walls he tried to get a hold, grappled for some way to climb up. Yelling, pleading with his brothers, they paid no attention. One of them laughed. "Let's see what will become of his dreams now!"

As time passed Joseph could hear them joking as they prepared their evening meal, and he could not believe what was happening to him. *Surely they won't leave me down here to die!* He cried out, "Please, my brothers, please. Don't do this to me!"

There was no use pleading. He slumped to the floor. *I guess they're going to kill me.* Something inside him rejected the idea. *They can't kill me because then my dreams would not come true.*

The aroma of the roasting lamb was tantalizing, and it had been some time since he ate the cheese and bread. *Surely they'll give me something to eat,* he thought. *I'm so thirsty!*

But they didn't.

"Look!" he heard one of them say, "Here comes some Ishmaelites. Midianites, too."

Joseph stood up, straining to hear what was going on. "What will we gain if we kill our brother and cover up his blood?" *That's Judah's voice,* he said to himself. "Come, let's sell him to the Ishmaelites and not lay our hands on him; after all, he is our brother, our own flesh and blood."

Joseph could feel his heart pounding. *Surely they won't sell me!* At the smell of water, the asses and camels were braying, and Joseph could hear them racing toward the wells. Above the ruckus of camel bells and barking dogs was the creaking of the well wheel, the splash of pouring water, and thirst tormented him.

About that time someone threw a rope into the cistern and commanded Joseph, "Hang on!" He didn't take it at once. The angry face of Judah peered down at him. "Grab it, Joseph, if you know what's good for you!"

"No!" he shouted.

"Then we'll stone you to death!"

Reluctantly Joseph took hold of the rope and held on as he was hauled up, bumping and banging against the side of the cistern. His brothers grabbed him and pulled him topside. "Please," he begged, but they answered by roughly shoving him toward the Ishmaelites.

"How much?" Judah asked of the traders.

The swarthy men looked at each other and smiled as if to say, "We have more slaves than we know what to do with."

The Ishmaelites had the same strong features as Joseph's brothers, with curly beards and leathery skin. "We are brothers," Asher whined, "sons of Abraham," as if that would matter.

The merchants, gathering their voluminous robes around them, shook their heads and smiled, amused at the brothers' attempts to outwit them. Condescendingly a Midianite offered, "Four asses," and grinned at the sport this afforded him.

Judah laughed. "You jest." And holding Joseph's arm, he said, "Not much muscle, I agree, but—," he laid his hand on Joseph's head. "He's strong up here!"

The beady eyes of a fat chieftain studied Joseph. "Too young. Too fearful. Too fair."

Joseph's brothers laughed again and, discounting the objections, paraded Joseph before them, showing him front and back. "Too young?" Judah asked mockingly. "He's seven-teen, old enough to marry. Too fearful? He trusts God and knows no fear. Too fair? Women find him handsome. Lithe and quick, he'll make a splendid slave. Worth a hundred shekels of silver in any market."

A be-ringed Midianite held up his fat hand and measured Joseph span by span. Leaning back he muttered, "One urn of Gilead balm, that's final."

"We don't need Gilead balm, we need good rams."

The arguing lasted far into the night. Not until the first light of day did the traders strike a bargain. Joseph, his head aching, wearily watched as the Ishmaelites carefully mea-sured twenty shekels of silver ingots in the scales. Judah held open the bag to receive the silver. "This will buy ten good rams," he said with satisfaction.

A youth no older than himself clamped an iron band around Joseph's neck and fit shackles on his ankles, taking no pains to avoid hurting him. Joseph wept and called out to his brothers, who were busy slaughtering a goat. Judah held up Joseph's cloak and began tearing it. "Splatter some blood on this," he told Asher.

On the long journey to Egypt, the manacles rubbing his neck and ankles raw, Joseph wept as he saw the green of Canaan give way to desert sand. Two merchants riding alongside him bragged about the bargain they had made. "A hundred shekels? That one will bring two hundred or more! Egyptians prize a Semite slave—they'll pay a fortune."

Ill most of the journey, Joseph could not retain the barley gruel made with rancid butter and hot peppers. He often fainted from the heat until a chieftain, seeing his unturbaned head, tossed him a wrapper and scolded the attendant. "Would you have us lose this slave? Take care of him or I'll have your filthy hide!"

The nights were no better than the days. The heat of the sun gave way to the chill of the night, and the wind blew incessantly. Afraid of robbers, the caravan stopped overnight in whatever protective cover the men could find where other flea-bitten troupes took refuge. Joseph was tormented by vermin crawling over his body and rats scurrying about. One night a windstorm brought sand that buried the baggage and filled the wagons. They lost three days digging out.

As they approached the border of Egypt, the caravan was required to stop at the forts guarding the Egyptian frontier. The Ishmaelites were clever about concealing contraband, and the Midianites, by their profuse flattery and generous bribes, paid little duty.

Joseph stared at the hairless border guards who wore body armor made of leather. In their two-man chariots pulled by well-kept horses, they looked invincible. As one of the soldiers inspected Joseph, he eyed him suspiciously.

A Midianite merchant, speaking half Egyptian and half Aramaic, was quick to explain. "Only a skinny youth. Worth nothing at all. An orphan I found in Dothan."

"A likely story, you thieving cutthroat." The soldier poked Joseph in the ribs. "Puny, but there's the light of intelligence in his eyes. Pharaoh's bodyguard is looking for a decent slave. The ones you've sold him before can't learn the language."

With a great show of humility the Midianite agreed. "I'll see that he gets this one."

"If he doesn't die first," the guard said.

Seeing that Joseph was ill and emaciated, the Midianite chieftain swore at the attendant, and with the flat side of his sword beat him about the buttocks. The boy broke and ran.

In a little while he returned bringing mutton stew, flat bread, and goat milk. As Joseph ate, the chastised youth taunted him, "I'll fatten you up only to bring a good price."

When at last the long train was nearing the city of Memphis, the chieftain called a halt, and lieutenants carried his orders the length of the caravan. Hearing the orders, the attendant went to work. Stripping Joseph, he poured water on his head to wash his dirt-caked skin. Joseph scrubbed his hair and face, washed his arms, legs, and body. Then the youth ordered him to shave off his whiskers, scant as they were. "How old are you?" the attendant asked.

"Seventeen."

"Hardly a man," he scoffed.

When Joseph finished shaving the guard doused him with strong smelling oil. "Lather yourself," he said and, tossing him a loincloth, "Put that on."

Arriving in Memphis in the confusion of the marketplace, the cacophonous babble of languages, Joseph followed his attendant and the Midianite through the crowd. Standing in the slave market were two slaves older than himself, their nearly naked bodies oiled, their necks like his encircled with iron bands. But Joseph was not put on the block. An official of some kind was standing there, and the chieftain bowed low. "Potiphar, captain of the guard," the official announced.

As Potiphar scrutinized Joseph, the Midianite extolled his attributes as a slave. As he prattled on, the captain, through an interpreter, asked Joseph, "Who are you?" to which Joseph answered, "I am a Hebrew, a son of Israel."

The captain turned about and jerked his thumb up, the sign that he would pay the price.

Joseph was taken to the servants' quarters on the ground floor of the captain's house. There he was outfitted in the worker's undergarment, a longer loincloth made of cotton. He was shown how to pull it tight across the back and pleat it in front like a skirt or apron. Then he was taken on a tour of the compound, and because his guide knew only Egyptian,

Joseph was left to understand only what his eyes and reason could tell him.

First he was taken outside where he observed that the house was surrounded by a wall and within the enclosure were formal gardens and a little pond. The house was square, made of mud brick, and had few windows. As they approached the entrance they passed through a chapel bearing images of humans with animal heads.

There was a central hall with dining room and bedrooms on either side, where, for the first time in his life, Joseph saw tables, chairs, and bedsteads. Stairs led onto the roof, where there was another garden.

He found that storerooms in the compound could only be reached by going through the living quarters of the house, a system to discourage theft, he supposed. Behind the house were sheds for slaughtering animals, a butcher shop, stables, and grain silos. There were also several workrooms adjoining the house. Bread baking and beer making occupied a number of men and women who shyly glanced at the new slave.

That night as Joseph lay on a goatskin pallet, he felt sick at heart. Alone in a strange land, *Will I ever learn their language?* he worried. He longed for his father's tent, his brother Benjamin, and the carefree life he once enjoyed. Covering his head with his arm, so weary he wondered if he would wake up, he thought about his dreams. *They will come true, I know, but how?*

In the days that followed, Joseph learned everything he could about the operations of the compound. He began by making bread. Women pounded barley in a mortar, then ground the kernels in a mill. Joseph and the men mixed the flour into dough. The dough was shaped into loaves and baked, after which some were sent to the brewery. To make beer, the loaves were mixed with water, mashed underfoot, and strained through baskets. The liquid then fermented in stone crocks.

Some days Joseph worked in the slaughterhouse, where he dressed pigeons, duck, and quail killed in hunting expeditions. Even the mess of slaves was excellent. In season there were vegetables and fruit as well as a variety of meats and poultry. Beer was the common beverage because wine had to be imported. Starved as he had been, Joseph ate hungrily. Observing Egyptian manners, he saw that each dish was served in a common bowl and eaten with the hands. He learned to reach in for a sample of stew or fish and, after eating, wash the hand in a basin.

Day by day Joseph's strength increased, his body filled out, and he felt energetic. Work was a challenge, and everything he did turned out well.

Constantly hearing the language and studying it by night, Joseph was encouraged by how quickly he learned enough to make himself understood. Fascinated with Egyptian writing, he practiced far into the night, making the intricate hieroglyphics.

Apparently pleased with Joseph's work, Potiphar began to take an interest in him and from time to time took him in his chariot to distant places. Once they went as far as the canal to observe irrigation systems.

In time, Potiphar made Joseph overseer of his entire estate, trusting him so much he seldom looked at his accounts. In his new position, Joseph had greater liberty to explore the city and surrounding environs. He was fascinated with the monuments to dead kings, the tombs and pillars, the massive art works.

The Egyptians' sense of beauty was strange to him. Women painted their faces with rouge and lip color, and after shaving their eyebrows, they painted almond-shaped marks above the eyes with a black kohl stick.

Potiphar's wife drew Joseph's attention to beauty treatments when he was passing through the house on his way to the storerooms. The first time he saw her sitting at her dressing table drawing the arch above her brows he was intrigued but quickly hurried on his way.

After that when Joseph had to go down the hall, he kept his eyes straight ahead. Some mornings Potiphar's wife called to him and, on the pretext of having him perform some task for her, detained him. In the Egyptian style, her tight straight dress bared half her body and did not reach the floor. Beautiful turquoise bracelets wound round her arms and the scent of her perfume was sweet as honey. With her long, slim fingers she often teased him, touched his face—trailed her henna-colored nails down his cheek. Embarrassed and afraid, Joseph got away as quickly as he could.

There was no other way to get to the storerooms except down that hall, and although Joseph kept his eyes straight ahead, the more he ignored her, the more aggressive she became.

As he lay on the goatskin at night, Joseph feared the fate he would suffer if Potiphar got wind of her attention. He did recall gossip among the servants about Potiphar's wife, gossip he had not paid attention to before. From their talk he knew a heathen man would take advantage of her advances, go along with her as the easiest way out. "She'll never tell," they'd say.

Tumbling and tossing, Joseph remembered his dreams. *Whatever happens,* he assured himself, *God's plan will be fulfilled. One day my brothers will bow down to me, and I will rule over them.* Faith in the promise eased his anxiety, and he was able to sleep.

The next morning Joseph had scarcely entered the hallway when Potiphar's wife called to him. "Come see the captain's divining cup."

Joseph dared not ignore her, yet he waited in the doorway for her to come to him. Dressed in only a dressing gown, the shape of her body was revealed in such a way he turned his face away. He felt her fingers on his chin turning his face back toward hers. Their eyes met, and Joseph felt trapped. There was a heady scent about her, and her full, red lips provoked a response in him he resisted. "The cup. You were going to show me the captain's cup," he prompted her.

"Oh, the cup. Yes, here it is," she said, reaching for the goblet. "His divining cup. Would you like to see how it's done?" There was water in the cup, and holding a small vial in her hand she dribbled a few drops of oil in the water. Leaning close to him she swirled the mixture around a few times, then watched it settle. Holding the cup so he could see inside, she spoke in a soft, intimate voice. "See the oily surface? The configuration of oil and water tells what the future holds."

"Oh?"

"Would you like to know what I divine?"

He could feel the trap tightening and tried to pull away. "You can't go yet." Swirling the mixture again, she "read" the configuration. "There is great pleasure awaiting my handsome servant—such pleasure as he has never known." She clutched his arm, and her breath was warm as she whispered, "Come to bed with me!"

Joseph shook his head. "With me in charge," he told her, "my master does not concern himself with anything in the house; everything he owns he has entrusted to my care. No one is greater in this house than I am. My master has withheld nothing from me except you, because you are his wife. How then could I do such a wicked thing and sin against God?"

She flung herself on the bed, sprawled there pouting, and Joseph jumped at the chance to get away. As he was closing the door she patted the bed beside her, the almond-shaped eyes begging him. Joseph shut the door and hurried down the hall.

Every day after that Potiphar's wife waylaid Joseph with the same proposition, and every day he refused. The more she tempted him the more he resisted her.

It was not long before the servants were aware of what was going on. Jealous as they were of Joseph's position, the men's coarse humor took on veiled references to the whole affair, and the women giggled at their remarks.

One morning as Joseph came into the compound, he was puzzled that everything was so quiet. *It must be that no one is about,* he thought. *That's odd. Is this some sort of trick?*

As he entered the hallway, Potiphar's wife was standing in the doorway waiting, a gleam of mischief in her eyes. In one swift move she grabbed him by the tunic. "Come to bed with me!" she demanded.

Joseph swiftly unfastened the tunic, slipped out of it, and ran out of the house.

In his quarters Joseph leaned against the wall to steady himself. Beads of sweat wet his forehead as he strained to hear if she was following him. *That scorned woman will—*

A bell was ringing summoning the household servants! Joseph watched as the servants came running out of their quarters to their assigned tasks in the house.

Later when they came out of the house they were bubbling with excitement. He overheard them say, "Left his tunic—not very smart." "Joseph . . . seduce his master's wife?" "Will the captain believe her this time?"

When Potiphar came home, he was hardly inside the door when his wife started screaming. For half an hour there was arguing and shouting, then all was quiet.

All night Joseph waited for his master's summons, but none came. *He will surely put me to death,* Joseph thought. And then he reconsidered. *No. If I am to rule my brothers, I cannot die. What then? Will he flog me? Strip me of my position? Or will he understand I'm unjustly accused?*

The next day Potiphar was waiting for him and, without looking him in the eye, condemned him to the prison in the compound where Pharaoh's prisoners were confined.

Joseph's cell was small, and the smell of urine was strong. In the days that followed, inmates told their stories of being high up in the government, then toppled by rival priests and politicians.

At night Joseph lay in the darkness, listening to the moaning and groaning of the other inmates. He decided to try to help. *If the warden will give me some soap and water, a broom, I'll scrub the cells, wash down the walls.*

Joseph's efforts greatly improved conditions; the warden was impressed and gave him other responsibilities. His performance convinced the warden that "his God is with him." And after observing him over a period of time, he made Joseph a trustee responsible for everything that was done in the prison.

Two new political prisoners assigned to Joseph had been taken into custody as the result of a plot to poison the king. One man had been the Pharaoh's cupbearer. Before he passed the cup to the king he would pour a bit of the beer in his palm and taste it. If he felt no ill effect he then placed the cup before Pharaoh.

The other prisoner was chief of the royal bakers. Joseph remembered working in Potiphar's bakery, and he decided that, if someone wanted to murder the Pharaoh, poison in the bread would be the best way, for it would be hard to detect.

On a visit to their cell Joseph found both men looking dejected. "Why are your faces so sad today?" he asked.

"We both had dreams," they answered, "but there is no one to interpret them."

"Do not interpretations belong to God? Tell me your dreams."

The cupbearer told him his dream about a vine and three

branches that produced grapes. "Pharaoh's cup was in my hand, and I took the grapes, squeezed them into Pharaoh's cup and put the cup in his hand."

Joseph smiled for God had told him what the dream meant. "This is what it means. Within three days Pharaoh will restore you to your position, and you will put Pharaoh's cup in his hand, just as you used to do when you were his cupbearer."

The cupbearer jumped up, hugged Joseph, and ran around the cell shouting. When he calmed down Joseph told him, "But when all goes well with you, remember me . . . mention me to Pharaoh and get me out of this prison. For I was forcibly carried off from the land of the Hebrews, and even here I have done nothing to deserve being put in a dungeon."

The chief baker spoke up. "I, too, had a dream," he said. "On my head were three wicker baskets of bread. In the top basket were all kinds of baked goods for Pharaoh, but the birds were eating them out of the basket on my head."

Understanding the meaning of the dream, Joseph hesitated, then spoke softly. "This is what it means. The three baskets are three days. Within three days Pharaoh will lift off your head and hang you on a tree. And the birds will eat away your flesh."

The baker became distraught and for the next three days cowered in a corner beside himself. On the third day the cupbearer was released. But the captain of the guard, Potiphar himself, came to the cell with an executioner, and they dragged the screaming baker to be hanged.

During the next few days Joseph waited expectantly, believing the cupbearer would speak the word that would bring his release. When the week passed and nothing happened, Joseph lost heart. He looked through the grating to the only patch of sky visible from the cell and wondered what God was doing.

Month after month went by with no change in the monotony of prison life. Two years passed before the cupbearer remembered Joseph. Joseph was reading to a blind prisoner when the warden rushed in and, unlocking the cell, told Joseph to come with him. "The Pharaoh wants to see you!"

Quickly Joseph followed the warden up the stairs. "First you must shave off your beard," he was told. "No man appears before the Pharaoh with a beard." The warden handed Joseph a razor and a mirror. It had been a long time since he had even trimmed his beard, and looking in the mirror, Joseph saw a lean, thirty-year-old man and scarcely recognized himself.

"Take off those prison clothes," the warden said. "Bathe yourself and put on this linen livery."

When Joseph was washed and dressed the warden led the way outside. Pharaoh's chariot was waiting and, with an armored charioteer at the reins, Joseph was whisked away.

Ushered into the palace, he was amazed at the splendor there—engraved bronze pieces, walls covered with murals, ebony images of Horus, alabaster jars, tables inlaid with ivory. Carved stone lions guarded the throne where Pharaoh was seated, surrounded by attendants and court officials.

The Pharaoh's headdress with its broad side pieces was made of gold and set with precious stones, and a wide gold collar was about his shoulders. His almond-shaped eyes appeared serpentine; the small square patch of beard on his chin was thick with wax. Bare to the waist, rolls of flabby flesh showed around Pharaoh's middle. Servants waved feathered fans over him, and a priest swung incense while Pharaoh sat holding a bejeweled scepter. On the finger of his right hand was the large signet ring with which he sealed official documents, and on his left arm was a gold amulet several inches wide, befitting the potentate of all Egypt.

Pharaoh addressed Joseph. "I had a dream, and no one can interpret it. But I have heard it said of you that when you hear a dream you can interpret it."

"I cannot do it," Joseph replied, "but God will give Pharaoh the answer he desires."

The Pharaoh leaned forward, and in a coarse voice told Joseph his dream about seven fat cows coming up out of the Nile followed by seven lean cows. The lean cows ate up the fat cows, yet their condition did not improve. The second dream he told was about seven heads of grain on a single stalk followed by seven other heads that sprouted but withered, blasted by the wind. The thin and withered swallowed up the seven heads of choice grain. "I told this to the magicians," he said, "but none could explain it to me."

Joseph opened his mouth and spoke confidently. "The dreams of Pharaoh are one and the same. God has revealed to Pharaoh what he is about to do." And he told him that the seven fat cows and seven good ears represented seven years of plenty; that the lean cows and poor ears represented seven years of famine that would follow. And he thought to himself, *Twice told, twice forewarned.*

The magicians looked at one another, chagrined that Joseph succeeded where they had failed.

The king was perplexed but looked to Joseph, not his officials.

Joseph told him, "And now let Pharaoh look for a discerning and wise man and put him in charge of the land of Egypt. . . . Appoint commissioners to take a fifth of the harvest of Egypt during the seven years of abundance. . . . This food should be held in reserve for the country, to be used during the seven years of famine."

Pharaoh fingered the scepter as he listened, and then he said, "Since God has made all this known to you, there is no one so discerning and wise as you. You shall be in charge of my palace, and all my people are to submit to your orders. Only with respect to the throne will I be greater than you." He stood up, removed his signet ring and put it on Joseph's finger.

Servants robed Joseph in fine linen. When he was dressed, Pharaoh hung a gold chain with a heavy medallion around his neck. "You will ride in the chariot as my second-in-command," the king told him.

Joseph bowed before the Pharaoh, overcome by the swift change of events. When he raised his head, magicians and court officials were bowing before him.

Pharaoh beckoned to the captain of the guard, and Potiphar summoned bodyguards to escort Joseph outside. There a chariot was made ready for him. The driver snapped the reins, and as they got under way, slaves ran ahead of Joseph shouting, "Make way! Make way!" People on the street stopped and stared at the new Grand Vizier.

In the days that followed, Pharaoh gave Joseph the name *Zaphenath-Paneah,* which means "Savior of the World." And he gave him a wife. "She's the daughter of Potipherah," Pharaoh told him.

Everyone in Egypt knew of Potipherah, priest of On, the city of the state temple. And Joseph had heard of his young daughter, Asenath, the child Potipherah dedicated to the god Neit. For political reasons Joseph, as Viceroy, must take this daughter as his wife because Egyptian balance of power between the priesthood and the government was held in check by intermarriage.

In time a son was born to Asenath, and Joseph named him Manasseh, a name that means forgetting, saying, "It is because God has made me forget all my trouble and all my father's household."

Joseph traveled extensively, from Memphis to Thebes, overseeing the commissioners responsible for collecting the fifth part of every harvest. In Cairo on the east bank of the Nile, he found lush gardens flourishing, narrow, winding streets, and colorful bazaars. To the west of Cairo he visited the Great Sphinx and the pyramids rising out of the desert at Giza. There he saw the sand dwellers, nomads who bred asses, sheep, and goats, eking out a bare existence.

He visited the delta and saw the possibility for a canal to link the river with the Red Sea. Water was precious in Egypt, and Joseph well understood the Egyptians' reverence for the Nile. Its regular flooding of the valley brought rich soil from the mountains and left it along the banks. The rest of Egypt was nothing but sand. Nor was there ever any rainfall. So precise was the timing of the flood, Egyptians devised a calendar by it. But in the years when the Nile did not overflow, there was famine.

During Joseph's administration, there were seven years of bountiful harvests with three crops a year. Surpluses were stored in granaries as well as the fifth portion required of farmers. There was such an abundance of grain, it was beyond measure, and Joseph stopped keeping records.

Before the seven years ended, Asenath gave birth to a second son whom Joseph named Ephraim and said, "It is because God has made me fruitful in the land of my suffering."

After the seventh year of plenty, the river Nile failed to flood. No silt was left along the banks, and the farming area returned to desert sand. Incantations and sacrifices were made by magicians and priests to no avail. Governmental underlings looked to Joseph for directions. They brought him his silver divining cup—silver because that metal was not found in Egypt, therefore, the most precious. The cup was engraved with religious phrases, names of deities, symbols, and Joseph's name as the Grand Vizier. A servant was preparing hot wax to drop in the water to form the configurations that would give answer to their questions.

Joseph waved the cup aside, then told them Pharaoh's

dreams and God's interpretation. "We have stored plenty of grain." They could not deny that God's provision for them during famine revealed his goodness and mercy.

Travelers brought news of drought in Canaan. Farmers there depended on two rainy seasons for a good crop, but no rain had fallen, and the second season was past. There was famine in other lands, but in the whole land of Egypt there was food.

When the Egyptians began to suffer, Joseph opened the granaries and began selling grain. Learning that there was grain in Egypt, famine-stricken people from Libya, Sinai, and Canaan came to buy food. During the second year of famine a delegation of ten men from Canaan arrived. Bowing before the Grand Vizier they looked up and astonished Joseph! There before him were Levi, Judah, Reuben, Asher, Issachar, Dan, Gad, Naphtali, Simeon, and Zebulun. *Where is Benjamin?* he wondered. Surprised and excited, he spoke to them in Egyptian. "Where do you come from?" and an interpreter quickly translated into Aramaic.

"From the land of Canaan," they replied, "to buy food."

No wonder they don't recognize me, he thought. *It's been more than twenty years—the last time they saw me I was only seventeen!* Then he remembered his dreams! *They are bowing down to me!* Desperate to get his wits together, he stalled. "You are spies! You have come to see where our land is unprotected."

The translator could scarce finish the accusation before the ten were protesting loudly. "No, my lord. Your servants have come to buy food. We are all the sons of one man. Your servants are honest men, not spies."

Honest men? I wonder. I'll put them to the test. He looked sternly at one frightened face after another. *They're older, heavier, but dressed the same—with beards. Here I am clean shaven, wearing this uniform—never would they expect me to be Egypt's Grand Vizier.*

Still stalling, he told them, "No! You have come to see where our land is unprotected."

They cringed before him. "Your servants were twelve brothers, the sons of one man who lives in the land of Canaan. The youngest is now with our father, and one is no more."

At the mention of his father and brother Benjamin, Joseph felt a lump in his throat. *But how can I know if they're telling the truth?* he asked himself.

As the interpreter finished translating, Joseph responded. "It is just as I told you: You are spies! And this is how you will be tested: As surely as Pharaoh lives, you will not leave this place unless your youngest brother comes here. Send one of your number to get your brother; the rest of you will be kept in prison, so that your words may be tested to see if you are telling the truth. If you are not, then as surely as Pharaoh lives, you are spies!" Turning to Potiphar he ordered the men taken into custody.

For three days Joseph left his brothers in prison in order to think through what he should do. *If I keep them all in prison and send only one back I may never know the truth about Father and Benjamin. They may be as wicked as ever, and anyone I might choose to send may never return.* Finally he decided to keep only one hostage.

Joseph called for the Hebrews and told them he was releasing all of them except one, but to prove that they were honest men they must bring their younger brother to Egypt or die. Pointing to Simeon, Joseph told Potiphar, "Take him back to the prison."

Relieved that they were not all being detained, the brothers bowed effusively and quickly gave money to the steward who took their sacks to the granary to fill. As they waited, they discussed their predicament, unmindful that Joseph could understand them. "Surely we are being punished because of our brother. We saw how distressed he was when he pleaded with us for his life, but we would not listen; that's why this distress has come upon us."

Reuben reminded them, "Didn't I tell you not to sin against the boy? But you wouldn't listen! Now we must give an accounting for his blood."

Hearing their remorse, Joseph could not control himself and left their presence to weep.

After he got control of himself, Joseph headed for the granary. He found the steward filling his brothers' order and told him to put the money they had paid for the grain in the mouth of each sack.

After a while, his brothers came to load their donkeys. As they led them out of the compound Joseph's heart went after them. *If only I might see my father's face, my brother Benjamin . . .* As the distance widened between them he choked back the tears. *God has kept his promise, my brothers have bowed down to me, but—*

Weeks and months passed, and every day Joseph asked the commissioners if the Hebrews had returned. The news from Canaan was that the drought was continuing, but there was no sign of his brothers returning.

Then one morning as the blazing sun came up over the horizon a steward brought Joseph word that the Hebrews had arrived. Joseph looked down on the compound, and there were his brothers straggling across the yard. Quickly Joseph counted them—eight, nine, ten! *Benjamin must be with them!* "Steward," he called, "Take these men to my house, slaughter an animal, and prepare a feast; they're to eat with me at noon." He was jotting down the seating arrangement. "Here," he said, and handed it to him. "Honor the last one on the list. Oh, yes, tell the captain to release their brother."

Joseph watched from the terrace as the steward rejoined the brothers. They were anxiously trying to explain something—*the money in their sacks.* Joseph smiled. Simeon came running across the yard, and they all embraced. Joseph could not tell which of them was Benjamin.

At noon Joseph and his bodyguards entered the house where his brothers were on their faces before him, holding gifts in their hands. So eager to see Benjamin, Joseph could hardly contain himself as a steward announced each present: "Honey, balm, spices, myrrh, pistachio nuts, and almonds." Joseph acknowledged the gifts and dispatched the servant to the kitchen with them.

Through an interpreter Joseph asked, "How are you? How is your aged father you told me about? Is he still living?"

They raised their heads, and Joseph spotted Benjamin. "Your servant our father is still alive and well," they answered and bowed again.

"Is this your youngest brother, the one you told me about?" And looking at Benjamin he said, "God be gracious to you, my son."

The sight of his brother, a young man with sidelong locks, deeply moved Joseph, and he had to leave the room.

In a little while Joseph regained his composure, washed his face, and rejoined his brothers. "Serve the food," he ordered, and seated himself alone at his table, the Egyptian officers at another table, and his brothers at yet another.

In a few minutes the brothers were surprised to find that they were seated according to their ages. When the food was served and Benjamin received five portions, they were even more perplexed. Joseph found it hard not to reveal himself, but he wanted further proof that they were honest men.

After the feast Joseph instructed the steward to do as he did before, put their money in their sacks, but, in addition, he told him to put his divining cup in Benjamin's sack.

As day was breaking Joseph's brothers loaded their donkeys and headed east on the long trek back to Canaan. Joseph allowed them to travel for an hour, then he sent his servant after them. "Go after those men at once, and when you catch up with them, say to them, 'Why have you repaid good for evil? Isn't this the cup my master drinks from and also uses for divination? This is a wicked thing you have done.'"

He watched as the steward mounted a camel and rode after them. *When the cup is found in Benjamin's bag the steward will demand that he return to face trial. If they allow Benjamin to bear the consequences alone, they are as they have always been. If that happens, the steward will bring Benjamin back, and I can protect him from them.*

All morning Joseph could not keep his mind on his work.

In early afternoon he stood at the window watching. Soon he saw the dust of travelers on the road. As they drew nearer he perceived them to be a small group. In a few minutes he could see they were his brothers—all of them! He could hardly keep back the tears as he realized they had not abandoned Benjamin.

Waiting for them in the royal parlor, he spoke harshly. "What is this you have done? Don't you know that a man like me can find things out by divination?"

"What can we say to my lord?" Judah replied. "How can we prove our innocence? God has uncovered your servants' guilt. We are now my lord's slaves—we ourselves and the one who was found to have the cup."

But Joseph refused to listen. "Far be it from me to do such a thing! Only the man who was found to have the cup will become my slave. The rest of you, go back to your father in peace."

The words distressed them. Judah stepped forward, earnestly explaining all that had passed between them and the Grand Vizier and how their father did not want them to bring Benjamin to Egypt. He quoted his father's words, "You know that my wife bore me two sons. One of them went away from me, and I said, 'He has surely been torn to pieces.' And I have not seen him since. If you take this one from me too and harm comes to him, you will bring my gray head down to the grave in misery."

Judah pleaded that their father would die if Benjamin were left behind, and he begged that he might stay in his stead.

Joseph could stand it no longer. "Leave me alone with these Hebrews," he told his attendants.

When they were alone, Joseph lost control, tears streamed down his face. "I am Joseph!" he cried. "I am your brother Joseph, the one you sold into Egypt!"

Judah gasped. The brothers turned pale.

"And now do not be distressed and do not be angry with yourselves for selling me here, because it was to save lives that God sent me ahead of you. God sent me ahead of you to preserve for you a remnant on earth and to save your lives by a great deliverance.

"So then, it was not you who sent me here, but God." Joseph took Benjamin in his arms and wept. Then he embraced the others mingling his tears with theirs.

Joseph told his brothers to go home and tell their father to bring all their family to Egypt. In time, the old man did come, limping as he came, and Joseph wept on his neck.

The Hebrews settled in the land of Goshen and prospered there. Jacob blessed the two sons of Joseph, thus giving him the birthright.

After the death of Jacob, Joseph's brothers feared that he would yet punish them for selling him as a slave, so they told him their father had left word that he was to forgive them. Joseph answered them kindly, "Don't be afraid. Am I in the place of God? You intended to harm me, but God intended it for good to accomplish what is now being done, the saving of many lives. So then, don't be afraid. I will provide for you and your children."

STUDY QUESTIONS

1. Do you think dreams have significance today?
   A. No, because now we have a completed Bible and revelation by dreams is unnecessary.
   B. Yes, if the person lives in a heathen country where there is no Bible.
   C. Yes. The Bible says that in the latter days old men will dream dreams and young men will have visions (Acts 2:17).

2. How is the providence of God shown in Joseph's life?
   A. By sending him into Egypt to save a great part of the world during famine, particularly the family of Israel.
   B. By providing a witness in Egypt of God's love and care.
   C. What was intended for evil, God used it for good.

3. From the reports of Christians interned in concentration camps, mental institutions, and prisons, is it possible that there are "Josephs" in the world today who will serve great purposes through their suffering?
   A. I think the experience of Joseph is unique in history and nothing quite like it will be repeated.
   B. The blood of the martyrs has been called the "seed of the church," and I do not believe anyone suffers for the cause of Christ without eternal purposes being served.
   C. God has no "favorite" children. Why can't we expect believers to suffer and serve the purposes of God even as Joseph did?

Something to Ponder: We would not know that Joseph's ankles were bruised with shackles and his neck put in irons if this were not revealed in Psalm 105. Is it not comforting to know that the Lord is equally as mindful of people of faith imprisoned today?

5

Moses

HE PERSEVERED BECAUSE HE SAW HIM WHO IS INVISIBLE.

Scripture: Heb. 11:27; Exod. 33:12–34:35

Joshua had climbed up Mount Nebo as far as the old man would allow him. Moses wanted to go alone to the top to view Canaan, the land promised to the Israelites, and Joshua must turn back. The two men were resting in the shade of a ledge before they would part. The younger man was overwhelmed by the responsibility that would soon fall on his shoulders, for Moses had appointed him to be the new leader of Israel.

For some time they talked about their experiences during the past forty years—particularly the difficulties in the desert.

"Tell me," Joshua asked, "with all the complaining, all the hardships of that great howling desert, what made you keep on?"

"You've asked me a question, Joshua, that I can answer. You wonder how I put up with all the complaining, with the ordeals we faced? Well, it was hard." He looked off toward the slopes of the higher range and spoke in a strong, resonant voice. "I was encouraged when I considered Abraham and the difficulties he went through. Promised this land that only now we are going to possess, Abraham kept on believing although he didn't live to see this day.

"I asked myself, 'What kept him going on?' He certainly saw no evidence the promises were going to be fulfilled. The only part of Canaan he ever possessed was the plot of land he bought for a burial ground. Abraham never had a permanent home; like us, he lived in tents all of his life. I concluded that Abraham looked for a permanent home that is invisible."

"You think that's what kept him going—that he thought of life as just a pilgrimage to a permanent home?"

"A place of God's making, yes, that and the promises of earthly blessing yet unseen. When it came to God's promises there Abraham trusted them implicitly."

"And that's what kept you going—your eye on an eternal home?"

"Well, yes, but God gave me something more."

As Moses reflected, his countenance changed; his eyes were unseeing, so deep in thought was he. Still absorbed, he began to relate his experience. "Do you remember that time I came down from Mount Sinai, and my face was shining in such a way you and the others could not look at me?"

"How could I forget?"

"Well, it all began one day when you and I went outside the camp to the tent of meeting. You remember that when I entered the tent the pillar of cloud would come down and stay at the entrance while God spoke with me?"

"And all the people would stand in the entrances of their tents and worship. Yes, I remember."

"On that particular day I was greatly distressed. The people had built the golden calf, and their sin had been severely dealt with. God told me we must leave Sinai and continue the journey to the Promised Land. I was worn out, defeated, and I didn't know how I could possibly carry on." Again Moses lapsed into a reverie.

Joshua prompted him. "What did you say to the Lord?"

He returned to the story, slowly quoting the conversation word for word. "You have been telling me," I said, " 'Lead these people,' but you have not let me know whom you will send with me. You have said, 'I know you by name, and you have found favor with me.' "

"What did he mean that he knows you by name?"

"He knows my character. A name stands for all a person

is. I said to the Lord, 'If I have found favor in your eyes, teach me your ways so I may know you and continue to find favor with you. Remember that this nation is your people.' "

"Did the Lord answer you?"

"Yes. He told me, 'My Presence will go with you, and I will give you rest.' His words I believed, but you must understand how desperate I was. I pressed him. I said, 'If your Presence does not go with us, do not send us up from here. How will anyone know that you are pleased with me and with your people unless you go with us? What else will distinguish me and your people from all the other people on the face of the earth?' "

"You were very bold, Moses."

"God did not rebuke me. In fact, he agreed to do exactly as I asked, because he said, 'I am pleased with you, and I know you by name.' "

"Did that satisfy you?"

"Not quite. Even though the Lord knew me intimately, I did not know him intimately. I was very bold. I asked, 'Now show me your glory.' "

"You asked *that!*"

Moses nodded his head and smiled. "The Lord did not rebuke me even for that. He said, 'I will cause all my goodness to pass in front of you, and I will proclaim my name, the Lord, in your presence.' "

Joshua scratched his head and tried hard to understand. "By his name he meant his character?"

"Exactly. Joshua, the Lord said, 'I will have mercy on whom I will have mercy, and I will have compassion on whom I will have compassion. But you cannot see my face, for no one may see me and live.' "

"How can anyone see him? He is invisible."

"I'm getting to that. God is invisible, but on occasion he has appeared to people. For instance, Jacob."

"When Jacob wrestled on the banks of the Jabbok?"

"The same. After the wrestling was over, remember he

said, 'I saw God face to face, and yet my life was spared'?"

"Yes, I remember. He did say that. But—"

"Well, Joshua, if there is a God, and we certainly know there is, isn't that what you would expect of him, not only that he would speak to us—whether by angel, by dream, or by voice—but also that he would reveal himself in person?"

"You mean come to earth?"

"Exactly."

"I guess you're right." Joshua considered the logic then looked up. "Well, go on with your story."

"After I asked to see God's glory, the Lord told me, 'There is a place near me where you may stand on a rock. When my glory passes by, I will put you in a cleft in the rock and cover you with my hand until I have passed by. Then I will remove my hand and you will see my back, but my face must not be seen.'"

"Where was this place?"

"On Mount Sinai. That was the last trip I was to make up the mountain. I was told to take two tablets of stone, for, as you know, I had smashed the first two. The Lord promised to rewrite his words on the tablets. He also told me to come alone. So, I chiseled out two stone tablets and did as I was commanded."

Moses was quiet, absorbed with the memory. There was about his countenance a brightness as if he was preoccupied with something awesome.

Finally, to break the spell of preoccupation, Joshua cleared his throat. "You were saying?"

"Oh, yes. As I hid in the cleft of the rock, God's cloud came down on the mountain, and his voice proclaimed his name." Moses' voice became excited. "He passed by in front of me, proclaiming, 'The Lord, the Lord, the compassionate and gracious God, slow to anger, abounding in love and faithfulness, maintaining love to thousands and forgiving wickedness, rebellion, and sin. Yet he does not leave the guilty unpunished; he punishes the children and their chil-

dren for the sin of the fathers to the third and fourth generation.' "

Moses stopped speaking, the words and revelation of God
profoundly moving him. And for Joshua the *Name* declared
in all its infinite meaning and worth excited in him such a
sense of worship he scarce could breathe!

"What I saw," Moses whispered, "was like the afterglow
of a sunset—the glory of the infinite, eternal God!"

His imagination greatly activated, Joshua was caught up
in the splendor of the vision. "What did you do, Moses?"

"I bowed face down on the ground and worshiped him.
'O Lord,' I said, 'if I have found favor in your eyes, then let
the Lord go with us. Although this is a stiff-necked people,
forgive our wickedness and our sin, and take us as your
inheritance.' "

"Did he answer?"

Moses nodded his head. "The Lord said, 'I am making a
covenant with you. Before all your people I will do wonders
never before done in any nation in all the world. . . . Obey
what I command you today. I will drive out before you the
Amorites, Canaanites, Hittites, Perizzites, Hivites, and Jebusites.'

"Remember this, Joshua—remember what he commanded." Moses clutched Joshua's arm and spoke intensely.
"God said, 'Be careful not to make a treaty with those who
live in the land where you are going, or they will be a snare
among you. Break down their altars, smash their sacred
stones, and cut down their Asherah poles. Do not worship
any other god, for the Lord, whose name is Jealous, is a
jealous God.' "

Silence hung between them for a long time.

"No wonder your face shone," Joshua murmured.

"I was never the same after that." Moses released his grip
on the younger man's arm. "So you see, Joshua, you have
nothing to fear. The Presence of God and all his name implies
goes with you as he went with us during all these forty years.

I saw the invisible Lord, and that kept me going. You, too, will succeed if always you envision the Lord who is unseen but ever present."

"You've written this in the book?"

"I have. You'll find the words where I left them."

STUDY QUESTIONS

1. Why do you think this experience was given to Moses?
   - A. Since the Israelites had just sinned in making the golden calf, Moses was at a very low ebb and needed it.
   - B. They were ready to leave Mount Sinai and the desert before them promised great hardship.
   - C. Moses would not have received the vision had he not been bold and persevering.

2. If you had a choice would you rather have a one-time experience such as Moses had or
   - A. Have the completed revelation of God in the Bible?
   - B. Have God the Father revealed to you through the Son?
   - C. Have the Holy Spirit present and teaching you now?

3. In the wilderness wanderings, Moses was able to endure because he saw "him who is invisible." In what way is this true of believers today?
   - A. In difficult times and in good times we are aware of the unseen Lord through reading the Bible.
   - B. Answered prayer assures us of God's presence.
   - C. We perceive the Lord in circumstances that give us his leading.

Something to Ponder: The various Hebrew names of God reveal his character to us today. Here are a few of them: *Elohim*, God's power; *Jehovah*, God's self-existence; *Adonai*, God as Master; *El Shaddai*, God who nourishes.

6

Rahab

BY FAITH THE PROSTITUTE RAHAB . . . WAS NOT KILLED.

Scripture: Heb. 11:31; Josh. 2 and 6:22–25; Matt. 1:5

The inn was empty of customers for the fear that gripped the city. All the soldiers were on alert and civilians were busy securing valuables. People huddled in the city square talking, some of them wringing their hands. "Look what they did to the Amorites!" a woman wailed.

"We know," a soldier answered. "Sihon and Og, with the strongest military defenses in these parts, cut down like chaff before the wind."

The women who plied their trade in the inn were jittery, and to keep them occupied, Rahab had them separating flax seeds from the stalks. She knew their minds were not on what they were doing for they made mistakes; they were consumed with fear of the vast horde of Israelites camped across the Jordan.

They talked bravely, trying to shore up their courage. "These double walls have protected the people of Jericho for centuries. They'd be foolish to try to take this city."

"The river's at flood stage. They can't possibly get across."

"Of course not. Especially with all those sheep and cattle."

"The cattle could swim," someone suggested.

"Not in that current. Besides—." Then the woman burst into tears. "Oh, what are we going to do?"

Rahab did not try to comfort her. It was no use, for the

woman knew what they all knew. "The river is no obstacle," Rahab told them. "Their God opened the Red Sea and let them pass over dry shod. By comparison the River Jordan is nothing, flooded or not."

"That happened forty years ago," one of the women said, sniffling in her apron, "before any of us were born. Perhaps it isn't true."

"It's true," Rahab said. "All the old people say it's true."

She got up from the stool and unlocked the window covering. One side of Rahab's house of ill fame was enclosed by the wall of the city, and the window opened high on the wall. Looking down over the tops of the palms growing in the Jordan Valley, she could see the thin trails of smoke rising from the Israelite camp in Shittim. The longing in her heart was a secret she had long kept to herself. When she was only a little girl her father had told her about the God who parted the waters of the sea, letting millions of his people escape from Pharaoh. The gods she knew could never perform such a miracle, and though she paid them tribute, ever in her heart was a yearning to know the God of the Red Sea.

One of the women, who kept going downstairs to hear what was going on in the city, returned with the news that additional troops were walking the wall and reinforcements were being built at the south gate.

Periodically, the king's men made proclamations in the city squares. "No one is permitted outside the city," they said. "Be advised the rationing of water is imminent."

When the streets seemed deserted and no customers came to the inn, Rahab explained, "Those men not on duty are in their homes or at the shrine praying. No man will come to the inn tonight."

A young girl shuddered. "This place is getting on my nerves. We might as well go somewhere else."

"Where will you go?" Rahab asked.

"I have a brother who'll take me in."

"And you?" she asked, looking at a thin, wasted woman.

"A friend—."

Satisfied that they did have places to go, Rahab followed them to the door. "Perhaps you'll be safer there than here," she told them.

For the next few days Rahab was alone in the inn, and she worried about her family. Young as they were, her brothers were in the militia, her elderly parents in the house of one of her sisters. Another sister was pregnant, and another was a widow with three little girls.

Standing in the doorway, Rahab watched the commotion on the street, heard the hysteria, and wanted no part of it. Closing the door behind her, she kept busy with the flax, collected all the seed, then put the stalks to soak.

For some time she occupied herself by weaving a rope from coarse yarn she had made from flax. *Somewhere in this house are the berries we picked last summer. If I can find them, I'll press the juice and dye this rope red.*

Every day the threat of invasion heightened, and the fate of Jericho, according to its citizens, was sealed. Rahab kept busy. From time to time she checked to see if the rotting flax was loosening the gums, letting the fibers separate from the stems, and she finished weaving the long rope. When there was nothing more to do she sat by the window looking down on the scene below. The broad river reflected the sun like a stream of copper winding through the trees. Unlike the panic-stricken citizens of Jericho, a gloom settled over Rahab. *I cannot bear to think I will die without coming to know the God of the Red Sea.*

She turned away from the window and tried to shake the gloom. *This flax is ready to be spread out to dry,* she told herself. And for the next hour she wearily climbed the steps to the roof, hauling the flax up there to dry in the sun.

The next day she was up early and ventured onto the street again. The word was the same—everyone frightened by the impending doom. Some of the women came by asking if they'd had customers. Rahab asked where the berries might be, but they did not know.

By afternoon, she was alone again and kept looking for the berry crock. When at last she found it, the sun was getting ready to set. Hearing a knock at the door, she hurried to see who it was. To her astonishment, two Israelite men stood there! She quickly brought them inside and looked up and down the street. No one was about that she could see. *Oh, dear me,* she thought, *a hundred eyes have seen them!* "Quick," she said, "follow me!"

The men obeyed, and she led them up the narrow steps onto the roof. "Lie down!" she ordered and rushed about scooping up armsful of flax to cover the spies. Piling the stalks on top of them, she quickly had them hidden.

Satisfied that they were as safe as she could make them, Rahab hurried back downstairs. *They'll come looking for them any minute,* she thought. Nervously, she took the crock of berries on her lap and began squeezing the juice from them.

Sure enough, in a little while soldiers were pounding on the door. Apologizing for her untidy appearance, she asked, "What may I do for you?"

"Two men entered your house. We've come to take them to the king."

"Yes, the men came to me, but I did not know where they had come from. At dusk, when it was time to close the city gate, the men left. I don't know which way they went. Go after them quickly. You may catch up with them."

Believing her, they rushed out of the inn and ran down the street. She watched to see which way they would go. *They're headed down the road toward the fords. They'll bolt the gate behind them.*

Rahab waited a few minutes, then slipped back up to the roof. As she uncovered the men, they sat up and brushed the straw off their clothing and their hair.

"Before you lie down to sleep," she said, "I've something

to tell you. I know that the Lord has given this land to you and that a great fear of you has fallen on us, so that all who live in this country are melting in fear because of you. We have heard how the Lord dried up the water of the Red Sea for you when you came out of Egypt and what you did to Sihon and Og, the two kings of the Amorites east of the Jordan, whom you completely destroyed. When we heard of it, our hearts sank, and everyone's courage failed because of you, for the Lord your God is God in heaven above and on the earth below.

"Now then, please swear to me by the Lord that you will show kindness to my family because I have shown kindness to you. Give me a sure sign that you will spare the lives of my father and mother, my brothers and sisters, and all who belong to them, and that you will save us from death."

"Our lives for your lives!" the Israelites assured her. "If you don't tell what we are doing, we will treat you kindly and faithfully when the Lord gives us the land."

Rahab cautioned them to go quietly back down the stairs where she had a place for them to sleep until it was safe for them to leave.

While the men lay down, Rahab resumed her work, soaking the rope in the berry juice, all the while thinking how she might help them escape. Getting past the guards and through the locked gates would be impossible.

But by the time Rahab hung up the rope to dry, she had devised a plan.

For a little while she herself nodded off but did not sleep soundly. Every time patroling soldiers came tramping down the street she woke up. Timing their regular patrols, she perceived the most favorable interval for an escape attempt. As the tramping footfalls faded from earshot, she decided, "Now."

Waking the men, Rahab said, "It's time to go."

In her hand was the newly made rope. She would use it to lower them through the window down the outside wall.

"Go to the hills so the pursuers will not find you," she whispered. "Hide yourselves there three days until they return, and then go on your way."

The grateful men cautioned her, "This oath you made us swear will not be binding on us unless, when we enter the land, you have tied this scarlet cord in the window through which you let us down and unless you have brought your father and mother, your brothers and all your family into your house. If anyone goes outside your house into the street, his blood will be on his own head; we will not be responsible. As for anyone who is in the house with you, his blood will be on our head if a hand is laid on him. But if you tell what we are doing, we will be released from the oath you made us swear."

"Agreed," she replied. "Let it be as you say." One of the spies tied the end of the rope to the stairs and tied the other end around his partner's waist. Helping the partner through the window, Rahab and the Israelite played out the rope as he needed it. Bracing his feet against the wall and holding onto the rope with his hands, he was slowly lowered to the ground outside the city.

Rahab and the other spy leaned their heads out the window, but, for the height of the wall and the darkness of the night, they could not see him standing below. The rope slack in their hands, they knew he had untied himself, and the Israelite hauled it up again. As he was tying the rope around his waist, he asked Rahab, "Do you think you can hold it?"

"I think so."

"Remember, now, when we come to take the city, let this red rope hang out your window."

She nodded. "Hurry."

He put his leg over the sill, took hold of the rope, and dropped over the side of the wall. The rope slid through Rahab's hands, burning both her palms, but she hung on. Struggling, she managed to wrap the rope around her arm and let it out little by little although the rope cut into her flesh. Straining as she was, it seemed to take forever for the spy to reach the ground. When at last the rope went slack in her hands, she caught her breath before hauling it up again.

After that fateful night, Rahab thought long and hard as to when and how she would tell her family so that their lives might be spared. *Not until the last minute,* she thought. *Otherwise I break my oath, and all else will fail.*

When the news came that Israel was crossing the Jordan River on dry ground, apprehension turned to panic. Women were weeping and wailing at the shrines, some running from one house to another, crazed with fear. Children were screaming. Rahab sat calmly by the window watching.

Weeks went by but with no letup of apprehension. Then the Israelite horde began marching toward the city of Jericho! Quickly Rahab uncoiled the rope and threw it out the window. As she looked down upon the Israelites approaching in the distance, they appeared as small as ants, but she knew the people of Jericho regarded them to be as formidable as giants.

The Israelites sounded no battle cry, only the blasts of trumpets heralded the approach. The sound was awesome, for the blare of trumpets praised the God of Israel, the God of the Red Sea.

Rahab ran down the steps, across the street and down an alley to her sister's house. Without explaining, she persuaded her parents and sister to come with her to the inn. After getting them inside Rahab went after her brothers, then her other sisters, until all her family were safe within her walls.

Seven days of marching passed before the assault came. Ram's horns signaled the attack, then there was a burst of battle yells. Simultaneously, a great rumbling shook the earth, walls cracked, teetered, and portions of them crashed. People were screaming, crying out to the gods while Rahab's family huddled together, trembling and waiting for what God would do. The thunder of collapsing walls and buildings was deafening, the inn shook, dust and smoke poured inside.

When the first wave passed, Rahab raised her head. "Everything's all right," she assured them. "The inn has not been damaged."

Soon the door burst open and Israelite soldiers rushed in the room. "Hurry!" they shouted. Grabbing up the children in their arms, they herded Rahab and the others outside.

Utter destruction was everywhere. The soldiers carefully steadied the elderly parents and the pregnant sister and, in all the confusion, led the way through the rubble, stepping over dead and mangled bodies. Heart-wrenching screams, anguished cries, and dying moans came from every side, but there wasn't a moment to waste.

They went past the main gate, now fallen in ruins, the second wall having fallen inward as well. They scrambled over great piles of debris to get away while Israelites were still climbing up the other side to get into the city.

Only when they were a safe distance from Jericho did the men stop. Breathless and pointing down the bluff, one of them told Rahab, "Follow that trail. It leads down to the fountains. Our women will take care of you. Tarry there until this is finished."

Rahab's brothers took the children, held onto the women's arms, and led them down the rough trail. With her father leaning heavily on her shoulder, Rahab looked back to see much of Jericho going up in flames.

STUDY QUESTIONS

1. How do you account for a harlot such as Rahab being interested in the God of the Red Sea?
   A. Her own gods and culture had brought her down to a life of debauchery, and she wanted something better.
   B. Fear was the motive; she wanted to save her life.

    C. Her conscience pained her. A God who could deliver a multitude could deliver her.

2. Do you think Rahab was converted?
    A. Yes, because there is a Rahab mentioned in the genealogy of Jesus (Matt. 1:5).
    B. I think so because in Hebrews 11 she is commended for her faith in saving the spies.
    C. Only God knows for sure.

3. Rahab lied to save the spies. Do you think that was a sin?
    A. Lying is always a sin.
    B. Lying in wartime to save lives is a part of the weaponry of war.
    C. She wasn't a believer when she told the lie so we can't assume that God approved.

Something to Ponder: The fact that Rahab and others remembered the crossing of the Red Sea, an event that had happened forty years before, proves the magnitude of that miracle. Don't you wonder how far-reaching was the news of that event in the known world of their day?

7

Deborah

I, DEBORAH, AROSE, AROSE A MOTHER IN ISRAEL.

Scripture: Judges 4 and 5

There was no unity among the tribes—Joshua was dead, and everyone went their own way, doing as they pleased. Contrary to God's command, the tribes had not exterminated the Canaanites but had left off fighting to cultivate the land and make themselves comfortable. If harvesting the crop meant breaking the Sabbath, they broke the Sabbath; if a son wanted to marry the neighbor girl, no voice was raised about her heathen religion. Grandchildren were brought up to worship their mother's idols. All sorts of forbidden alliances were made—partnerships, compromises, all in the effort to become wealthy gentry riding on expensive white donkeys. Lawlessness prevailed. Crime was rampant.

Deborah grieved that the roads were not safe to travel; to go anywhere a traveler chose the back roads or a little used path. Even then criminals often found their prey. People were afraid to gather at village wells for fear of attack, robbery, or rape.

Israel's disregard for God and his commands provoked his judgment; Canaanites overpowered the Israelites and made them subservient for twenty years. The Canaanite king was known by the royal title of Jabin and reigned from Hazor. Sisera, the great general who led the formidable Canaanite army, lived in Harosheth near Mount Carmel and took pleasure in the cruelties he inflicted on the Israelites. Whatever the oppressors demanded they received, for the Israelites had no weaponry to match the Canaanite chariots, their long-bow marksmen, their protective coats of mail, iron helmets, spears, and shields.

Deborah, called by God to be a prophetess, counseled the people in a palm grove in the tribe of Ephraim, situated between the towns of Ramah and Bethel. That hill country had been hard won, for faith in God had waned. Perceiving Bethel as difficult to conquer, the Israelite tribe of Ephraim had conquered Bethel by promising to spare the family of the Canaanite who betrayed the city into their hands.

"Neither then nor now," Deborah complained to her husband, Lapidoth, "has there been a statesman in Israel."

"Are you forgetting Othniel, Ehud, and Shamgar?"

"Judges, Lapidoth, judges. What the country needs is a leader like Joshua—a man of God who will hold the people to the Word of God."

"I see," he said lamely but showed no desire to become involved.

The oppressed people came in droves to Deborah with their disputes and for counsel and prayer. God gave her wisdom and compassion, but as well as comforting the Israelites in their affliction, Deborah rebuked them for their disobedience. "You sinned when you married him," she told the wife of a brutal man. "God told us not to make marriages with inhabitants in the land. He's a Hittite. What did you expect?"

But there was the gentler side of her. Children followed her everywhere, gathered around her to hear the lovely melodies she played on the lute. Sometimes she sang to them a ballad of her own composition or a song of Moses. The singing was to encourage them, to evoke praise to God for his exploits on behalf of the people of God, but the children had seen so little of the power of God in their short lives it was difficult for them to believe. They looked up at her with sad eyes, eyes that lacked the joy and innocence of childhood.

Yet the children were the first to begin crying out to the Lord for help. Their simple prayers were honest and to the point, heart-wrenching for the pain expressed. "My father is dead, and my mother is sick. The Canaanites took my brother, and I am left alone."

"Sisera's men took all our food. Oh, Lord, help us as you helped Joshua."

But it was not until their parents took up their cry that God began to answer. The Lord revealed to Deborah what she should do. She sent a messenger to Barak, a promising leader of the tribe of Naphtali who lived in Kedesh, asking him to come at once.

Waiting under the palm tree, Deborah strummed a song for the children, but her thoughts were on Barak and what God had revealed. *God has chosen Barak, no stronger than any other man, and me, a woman with no art for battle, to win the victory.* The thought humbled and excited her. *After all these twenty years once again God will show his hand, and we shall be free.*

The next day Barak arrived. Deborah took him aside and told him, "The Lord, the God of Israel, commands you: 'Go, take with you ten thousand men of Naphtali and Zebulun and lead the way to Mount Tabor. God will lure Sisera, the commander of Jabin's army, with his chariots and his troops to the Kishon River and give him into your hands.' "

Color drained from Barak's face. He sat down quite unable to believe what he had heard. Finally, he spoke. "If you go with me, Deborah, I will go; but if you don't go with me, I won't go."

Deborah was disappointed. *Still leaning on the arm of flesh,* she thought. *Or worse, treating me as one who has the oracles of God, a good-luck charm such as the heathen trust.* "Very well," she said. "I will go with you. But because of the way you are going about this, the honor will not be yours, for the Lord will hand Sisera over to a woman." That a woman would defeat Sisera, the gallant warrior, mighty general, would be thought incredible.

Barak managed a weak smile, and Deborah mounted her donkey for the trip to Kedesh.

When they arrived in Naphtali, word spread quickly that Deborah had come. Mustering a militia from the tribes of Naphtali and Zebulun was made easier because she was there. Men trusted the word of the prophetess. In a matter of weeks, ten thousand volunteers were assembled. Pitifully armed with slings, short-range bows, bronze daggers and swords, the men of Israel knew they were no match for the well-equipped Canaanite army with its nine hundred iron chariots, thousands of trained soldiers, expert archers and charioteers.

"What of the other tribes?" the recruits asked.

"The call to arms went out to all the tribes," Barak replied. "Benjamin filled their quota, as you can see, and Ephraim sent troops. Men of Issachar are here. But the Reubenites did not come. At first they considered joining our ranks—thought long and hard, I understand—but in the end chose rather to stay by their flocks."

The news met with jeers. "What about Israelites beyond the river?" someone yelled.

"Gilead stayed where they are."

"And our seacoast brothers?"

"Asher and Dan chose to stay by their ships in the safe harbors and coves," Barak reported.

"Come along," Deborah prodded. "Sisera is ready to do battle."

Deborah marched with the troops all the way to Mount Tabor. Small clouds like a flock of sheep paraded across the sky. The sun was warm, and along the way wildflowers carpeted the field with a lavender haze. *This is a day that will long live in the history of our people*, she thought.

As they approached the mountain, the smooth curve of its

crest gave it the appearance of a bowl turned upside down. As they climbed up the north side, Deborah knew that at the crest of the mountain the men would see what they had never seen before—an overpowering battle array. She was one of the first to reach the top and, dropping to her knees alongside the men, she gazed down at the Kishon River plain alive with horses and chariots rolling into formation; thousands of rank-and-file foot soldiers at ready, their shields and spears gleaming in the sun; color bearers, their banners waving; shouting commanders; blasts of trumpets; horses neighing—!

Frightened, Barak turned to Deborah. She told him, "As I said, we march down the mountain toward them. The sight of us will lure them onto the field, and God will give us the victory."

Barak passed the word, the ram's horns carried the order to the last man. Barak yelled, "Charge!" and started down the mountain.

Immediately the enemy responded, moving full speed toward them. The chariots, rapidly approaching the Kishon River, were followed by Canaan's marching troops. On and on they came, an unbroken line, rank on rank, never faltering, never slackening their steady pace.

The men of Israel were yet a distance from the enemy when Sisera's chariots reached the river. Suddenly there was panic! The heavy iron chariots were bogging down in the mud. Then suddenly, just as the chariots were caught in the path of the river, out of nowhere flood water was rushing into the valley. The wild frenzy of horses—cries of trapped men—bedlam! Troops broke ranks and deserted comrades, only to be swept away by the rushing water.

Seeing some of the chariots headed toward Harosheth, Barak ordered his men to pursue. Other Canaanites were fleeing on foot or trying to commandeer a horse. Sisera abandoned everything and ran.

But Sisera was not to escape.

The next day Deborah received word that Jael, a woman

married to a Kenite, had killed Sisera. Believing the Kenite family friendly to his king, Sisera sought refuge in Jael's tent. She played upon his confidence, showed him the usual courtesies, gave him curdled milk to drink, and put him to bed in the women's quarters where no one could intrude. Then, when he was fast asleep, she took a tent stake, its point sharpened to penetrate the rocky soil. Putting it to Sisera's temple, she made one swift blow that ended his life.

Canaanite power was broken! Israel's tribes were free. A great celebration followed the victory. Deborah wrote a ballad telling the story. Gathered around a bonfire, she and Barak sang the song accompanied by instruments played by the troops. Verse after verse described conditions in Israel until, "I, Deborah, arose, arose a mother in Israel."

Cheers resounded at the words.

Stanza after stanza revealed all that led up to the battle, the action taken, the results. And the crowd joined in the refrain:

> Wake up, wake up, Deborah!
> Wake up, wake up, break out in song!
> Arise, O Barak!
> Take captive your captives, O son of Abinoam.

It was a song sung for many years afterward—sung when women gathered at village wells and recounted the righteous acts of God. Sung by women of faith living in troublesome times when a "mother in Israel" was needed.

STUDY QUESTIONS

1. Can you think of similarities between Deborah's time and ours?
   A. People did as they pleased.
   B. People were afraid to travel on public roads.
   C. There was little respect for God's commands.

2. Is there any sense in which women today play a role like Deborah's?
   A. Yes, as counselors, teachers, governmental leaders, and so forth.
   B. No. There's no such thing as a woman prophetess today.
   C. Because of the sinful time in which she lived God permitted Deborah to take the lead, and she is unique in history.

3. Do you think Jael was right in killing Sisera?
   A. It was murder. She deceived him and took advantage of him while he was asleep.
   B. How could a weak woman kill a soldier without taking advantage of him?
   C. It was predicted that a woman would kill him so it must have been approved by God.

Something to Ponder: "A mother in Israel" is a beautiful phrase. Can you think of other women in the Bible or in our time who would qualify for the title?

8

David

YOU COME AGAINST ME WITH SWORD AND SPEAR AND
JAVELIN, BUT I COME AGAINST YOU IN THE NAME OF THE
LORD ALMIGHTY . . . WHOM YOU HAVE DEFIED.

Scripture: 1 Samuel 17

From David's earliest recollection he had always admired the expert warriors who fought with slings. The members of a crack unit from Benjamin were left-handed and with their slings could without fail hit a mark the width of a hair's breadth. Some of them used either hand and were equally accurate. But no matter how much he practiced, David was never good at it.

The two straps of the sling were cut from rawhide, and he was careful to match their width and length precisely so the stone would be balanced in the pouch. He had learned to choose smooth stones so they would not veer away from what he was aiming at, but he had never mastered the skill of slinging stones. There was a knack to throwing the sling to get the maximum thrust, and David, being slight of build, did not have the strength to power the thrust. His stones usually fell short of their targets. Discouraged, he gave himself to playing the lute, something he excelled in.

David's musical talent had taken him to Saul's court, where he played soft music to calm the king's nerves. The experience gave him insight into what kind of life he might have in the future. Although he dared not speak of it, the prophet Samuel, acting at God's command, had come to Bethlehem in secret and anointed David to be the next king of Israel. Honored as he was to be chosen, David put the prospect out of his mind because he much preferred his life as a sheepherder. In fact, he liked everything about that life—lambing time, shearing time—except the slaughtering. The bond between shepherd and sheep was such that a man would give his life to save his flock.

Because of his lack of skill with the sling, David depended on his rod to defend the sheep. At close range he could hurl the club end over end and hit the jackal or fox chasing the sheep.

Since his three older brothers had gone off to war, David was often alone in the fields of Bethlehem with one of his father's flocks while his other four brothers were grazing their sheep in other pastures. Only a few hired men helped him, and they were not fully responsible. Wild animals usually attacked at night when the sheep were in the fold. David counted the sheep as they entered the fold, then lay down across the entrance. But he did not sleep soundly. There was always the danger that a wolf would climb over the enclosure. At the first bark of one of the dogs, David would be on his feet, rod in hand, ready to drive off the predator. Sometimes the threat came from within the fold—snakes or lizards often crawled out from under rocks and excited the sheep.

As a boy growing up in the fields David had learned to distinguish sounds of harmless creatures from those that were dangerous. He knew the night sounds of owls and hyenas and of ground creatures scurrying about. But the telltale snap of brush or bramble would alert him even before the first dog barked, aware as he was of the cunningness of leopard or lion. He was particularly on guard when the River Jordan was in flood stage because, as the river rose, the lions were forced to leave their lairs in the valley and roam about the hills.

Usually the dogs chased animals away, or if a shepherd was good with a sling he could stone them at long range. But when the shepherd lost—sheep were killed, and sometimes shepherds were injured, even killed.

David had experienced more than one encounter with attackers, not only lions but bears. When a lion sneaked up behind the flock and carried off a sheep, David went after him, hit him with the rod and while the beast was stunned, took the sheep from its mouth. As he headed back to the flock, the lion turned on him, and David, with his bare hands, took hold of the lion's mane and mauled it with the club until it was dead. In somewhat the same way he had killed bears.

Even that big she-bear—I killed that one, too, he reminisced, awed by the supernatural strength given to him. *Not a human feat,* he told himself for the hundredth time. *The Lord delivered me every time.*

Whistling to the dogs, David decided it was time to lead the flock home.

David's father, Jesse, was waiting for him at the stable and patiently stood by as the sheep were corraled into the confines of the old cave. Leaving the flock in the care of hired hands, David walked with his father toward the house. "I want you to go and see about your brothers," Jesse told him. "I'm afraid Saul's troops are no match for the Philistines."

They sat down in the courtyard, and David listened as his father talked. "David, before you were born, Saul showed great tactical skill at Michmash. In that battle he routed the Philistines with such a smashing defeat they have posed no threat to us until recently. But now Saul is floundering, unable to cope with the overpowering Philistine army." The old man laid his hand on David's shoulder. "I want you to go and see how things are going at the battlefront—how your brothers are faring."

"Very well, father."

Early the next morning David loaded ten cheeses, roasted grain, and ten loaves of bread on a donkey and headed for the

Israelite encampment in the Valley of Elah. The valley was situated opposite Ephes Dammim between Socoh and Azekah, where the Philistines were assembled. When David arrived, he saw the battlelines drawn, but no action was taking place.

Leaving the supplies with the quartermaster, David ran to the lines and found his brothers, Eliab, Abinadab, and Shammah. "Father is concerned about you," he said. "We've heard nothing of the battle."

His brothers exchanged looks and remained silent. David looked across the wadi at the Philistine hosts armed to the teeth. In a few minutes a giant of a man stepped out from the enemy ranks, and as he did the men of Israel ran back away from him, frightened out of their wits. David stood his ground and watched as the Philistine stalked up and down. The giant's bronze helmet, catching a sun's ray, was flashing as if lighted. The helmet looked like metal feathers held by a band around the head with scale armor attached, which protected the neck and sides of his face. The massive chest was covered with metal plates held in place by shoulder straps. Metal greaves protected his legs and ankles, and a strap across his chest held a circular frame for the shield carried on his back. A sword to fit his size hung in its scabbard, and armor bearers followed the giant, carrying a spear and a javelin about five feet long.

For a while the giant shouted insults at the army of Israel to the applause of his comrades. His abuse and insolence were offensive, but the cowardice of Israelite soldiers made David ashamed. With great bravado the giant boasted of his prowess and the might of the Philistines.

"I'd say he's spoiling for a fight," David remarked to the water boy.

"He wants a battle of champions rather than full-scale battle."

The challenger's booming voice reverberated between the hills. "Why do you come out and line up for battle? Am I not a Philistine, and are you not the servants of Saul? Choose a man and have him come down to me. If he is able to fight and kill me, we will become your subjects; but if I overcome him and kill him, you will become our subjects and serve us."

"Why doesn't someone fight him?" David asked.

"Ha! Do you know how tall that man is? He's nine feet four inches!"

"So? What is that to God?"

The water boy looked at him curiously. "He's Goliath; you've heard of him."

Of course he had, but no giant made him tremble. David rejoined his brothers who were with a group of soldiers hiding in the brush. He asked them, "What will be done for the man who kills this Philistine and removes this disgrace from Israel?" At first no one answered him. To Eliab's annoyance David insisted, "Who is this uncircumcised Philistine that he should defy the armies of the living God?"

Ignoring his indignation, one of the soldiers replied, "The king will give great wealth to the man who kills him. He will also give him his daughter in marriage and will exempt his father's family from taxes in Israel."

Goliath was shouting again. "This day I defy the ranks of Israel! Give me a man and let us fight each other."

David looked at the Israelites and shook his head in disbelief, condemning their cowardice. Eliab's face flushed. "Why have you come down here?" he demanded. "And with whom did you leave those few sheep in the desert? I know how conceited you are and how wicked your heart is; you came down only to watch the battle."

"Now what have I done?" David answered disgustedly. "Can't I even speak?" He turned away from his brothers and started talking to other men. "I'll fight him," he said. Someone who heard him reported his willingness to Saul.

Saul sent for David but taking one look, his disappointment showed. David said to the king, "Let no one lose heart on account of this Philistine; your servant will go and fight him."

Saul replied, "You are not able to go out against this Philistine and fight him; you are only a boy, and he has been a fighting man from his youth."

But David insisted. "Your servant has been keeping his father's sheep. When a lion or a bear came and carried off a sheep from the flock, I went after it, struck it, and rescued the sheep from its mouth. When it turned on me, I seized it by its hair, struck it, and killed it. Your servant has killed both the lion and the bear; this uncircumcised Philistine will be like one of them, because he has defied the armies of the living God. The Lord who delivered me from the paw of the lion and the paw of the bear will deliver me from the hand of this Philistine."

Saul walked up and down the room a couple of times then snapped his finger at a bodyguard. "Clothe this man in my tunic and armor. Get a helmet for his head."

David tried on the paraphernalia—the bronze helmet heavy on his head, the sword sagging at his side. The tunic was too big for him, the coat of mail clumsy and ill-fitting. "I cannot go in these," he told Saul, "because I'm not used to wearing armor."

Saul sighed, shook his head, but told David he could take off the armor. The bodyguard helped him remove it, and in his shepherd's garb David left the king for the contest.

As he approached the battle scene, David thought about the weapon he should use. *I'd like to use the rod, but if I did I'd have to wait for him to come within range. Surely he will strike before coming that close. I'd better use the sling,* he decided.

At first Goliath did not see David approaching, but when he did, he headed toward him. Using his shepherd's stick, David walked steadily down the hillside to the stream that ran along in the valley. Wading in the water he reached down and picked up several stones, selected five that were smooth, and slipped them in his bag.

With his shield bearer in front of him, Goliath's body was well protected as he kept coming closer. *He has the advantage,*

David thought. *He has the high ground. Slinging a stone from down here will lose some force.*

When the giant was near enough to see that David was only a boy with just a stick, he was insulted. "Am I a dog, that you come at me with sticks?" And he cursed David by his god Dagon. "Come here," he yelled, "and I'll give your flesh to the birds of the air and the beasts of the field!"

David was quick to answer, his reedlike voice shrill, "You come against me with sword and spear and javelin, but I come against you in the name of the Lord Almighty, the God of the armies of Israel, whom you have defied. This day the Lord will hand you over to me, and I'll strike you down and cut off your head. Today I will give the carcasses of the Philistine army to the birds of the air and the beasts of the earth, and the whole world will know that there is a God in Israel!" He paused to shout louder. "All those gathered here will know that it is not by sword or spear that the Lord saves; for the battle is the Lord's, and he will give all of you into our hands."

The infuriated Philistine charged down the hill, and David, fumbling in his bag for a stone, got ready. Fitting the stone in the pouch he began swinging the sling around and around over his head. Goliath kept coming, roaring as he came!

As David swung the sling overhead—*swoosh—swoosh—swoosh*—he whipped it faster and faster. *Once more,* he told himself and then *let it go!* The stone left the sling like a thunderbolt, struck the giant in the forehead, and sent him sprawling headfirst! David ran up the slope where he lay. Pulling Goliath's sword from its scabbard, he began hacking off the giant's head.

As David triumphantly held up the massive head, the Israelite army roared with cheers and surged down the hill chasing the panic-stricken Philistines.

David watched as Israelites slaughtered their enemies. Philistine bodies were being strewn all over the mountain as Israel pursued the fleeing army.

David returned to Jerusalem, taking the head and Goliath's weapons with him. Saul's captain, Abner, met him and ushered him in to the king. "Whose son are you?" Saul asked.

"I am the son of your servant Jesse of Bethlehem."

The news of victory spread rapidly. By the time the Israelite army was returning from the battle, women from all the towns around came out to meet the soldiers, singing and dancing, accompanied by tambourines and lutes. As they danced, they sang, "Saul has slain his thousands, and David his tens of thousands."

The song troubled David. *Do they not understand? It is the Lord who saved us; for the battle is the Lord's. He did it, not I. If they only knew how unskilled I am with the sling—"*

STUDY QUESTIONS

1. In the final analysis, did David's expertise in defending sheep have anything to do with killing Goliath?
   A. Yes. It convinced Saul to let him try.
   B. No. David killed the lion, the bear, and the giant only by the power of God.
   C. The fact that he had killed the animals gave David faith to believe he could kill Goliath.

2. Are there foes in the Christian life as formidable as Goliath was to Israel?
   A. Yes. Our warfare is not against flesh and blood but a spiritual battle against all the Devil's temptations.
   B. Christians imprisoned for their faith are encountering political systems of gigantic proportions.
   C. The Giant of Despair threatens some Christians.

3. In what way is the Christian "army" of the living God defied today?
   A. By philosophies that deny God and threaten our educational and political systems.
   B. By cults whose members zealously spread false teaching.
   C. By the "armies" of rampant drug dealers who vigorously seek to seduce.

Something to Ponder: Although the defeat of Goliath was a miracle, David had to sling the stone. When Christians face a "giant" of some kind today, how do they know what is their part in the matter and what is God's part?

Part II

New Testament Examples

9

Anna

SHE SPOKE ABOUT THE CHILD TO ALL WHO WERE LOOKING
FORWARD TO THE REDEMPTION OF JERUSALEM.

Scripture: Luke 2:21–38

Simeon was a trader dealing in crockery, pottery jars, wooden plates, and cooking pots. Every weekday found him at his stall, peddling his wares. With industry and thrift he managed to feed and clothe his family and have enough money to set aside for unforeseen needs.

Despite his business, Simeon, in the prime of life, energetically pursued his spiritual inclinations so that prayer was like breathing to him, devotion to God surpassing all other commitments. So engaged was he in studying the Scriptures, in distributing to the needs of every drunkard, fallen woman, or orphan he could find, there was little time for cultivating a social life or conventional pleasures. Some people criticized him, calling him an eccentric and, in some instances, a fanatic. But the man was indifferent to either praise or scorn, so the criticisms fell on deaf ears.

In his quiet way, Simeon's faith was robust, thriving on the Scriptures and on the many opportunities given him for serving others. When he was not tending his shop or caring for his family, he was poring over the prophets or worshiping in the Temple or seeking out the beggars who frequented the Temple steps.

One of Simeon's closest friends was an old prophetess whom he had known since boyhood. She had taught him much when he was growing up. Her name was Anna, and now that he was a believer in his own right, they shared answers to prayer, the needs of others, and their expectations. Everyone in Jerusalem who came to the Temple knew Anna, for she was there day and night, praying and prophesying. And as she had encouraged Simeon, so she encouraged many others in their spiritual struggles.

"She reminds me of Deborah," Simeon told his wife. "Like Deborah, she counsels a generation living in very dark days. Let a man be mistreated by the authorities, and Anna is right there helping him through the ordeal. Let a woman lose a baby in childbirth, and she'll be there comforting her, bringing her nourishing food and praying with her."

"She's very frail," his wife said. "She fasts too much."

"She's never sick."

"But at her age—"

"How old do you think she is?" Simeon asked.

"Well, let's see. She was married seven years, my mother said, then her husband died."

"Let's say she married at fifteen—"

"She's in her eighties. Why don't you ask her?"

Simeon had better things to talk about with Anna. He had been reading the prophecy of Daniel, and like other students of Scripture, he had come to the conclusion that the Messiah would soon put in his appearance. *If only I might live to see him,* he often said.

Then one day he was given the solid assurance that he would live to see the coming of the Christ. Before he told anyone else, he thought, *I must tell Anna!* and rushed to the Temple—flying up the steps two at a time.

Pushing his way through the milling crowd, Simeon looked for Anna in the courtyard where money changers were holding forth, but she was nowhere about. Then he searched the women's court, and in a few minutes he spotted her diminutive figure sitting by a pillar over against the treasury.

Three young women were talking with her, and Anna was listening so intently she was oblivious to the Sadducees parading themselves like peacocks. Sadducees tried to outdo one another in giving to the Temple. Each man brought along a slave to carry his money, and as he proceeded past the thirteen receptacles for collections the slave poured in the gifts of his master. Admirers blocked Simeon's way. *They won't let me through,* he told himself. *I'll have to go around.* As he skirted the crowd, bursts of applause signaled every contribution.

In a few minutes, breaking out of the crowd, Simeon impatiently interrupted the three women and tugged at Anna's sleeve. She looked up. "You're late," she said.

"I know. The Lord detained me!"

"Oh?"

Simeon took both her hands in his and helped her to her feet. "Wait until you hear what I have to tell you!"

Suspecting the nature of his news, Anna's skin, transparent as parchment, took on a glow he had often seen on her dear old face. Simeon reached for her cane, saw that she was steady, then drew her aside where they could talk and not be overheard. Speaking in her good ear, he confided, "God has told me I will live to see the Messiah come!"

She was not surprised. "The Messiah?" she repeated softly, cherishing the sound of the name.

"Yes. Remember, we thought he must come soon because of Daniel's prophecy? But now the Spirit tells me that I will live to see him!"

"But will I?" she asked.

Simeon could not answer. Changing the subject, he said, "My wife's been worried about you, Anna. Are you eating? Do you stay warm?"

There was a twinkle in her eye, "Do I look like I'm tired of living?"

Simeon laughed. "No, you don't. But do you eat right?"

"I've no teeth for solid food. A little broth, some bread— God keeps me healthy."

"Here, take my arm. Let me take you home."

"You know I don't leave the Temple, Simeon. I have work to do."

The next morning by the time Simeon was able to get to the Temple, Anna had spread the word. He first realized it when a fat woman with three children in tow met him on the Temple steps and asked, "Is it true?"

When Simeon found Anna he scolded her. "Anna, what do you mean telling everyone our secret?"

"What secret? God's truth is for everyone!" It was her turn to scold him. "We have always known that the Messiah will appear in his Temple, and haven't we been telling those who believe that he will come soon?"

"But it may be years yet."

"Hardly. I think it could be any day now. A traveler from Bethlehem told me about angels visiting shepherds to tell them Messiah has come."

"Will angels visit us? How will we know him, Anna?"

"The same Holy Spirit who spoke to you will tell us, Simeon. Now sit here beside me, let's look for him."

As they sat watching people come and go, Anna hummed to herself as was her habit, interrupting herself only to call one friend after another over to the pillar to tell them the good news. "The Lord has told Simeon he will live to see the Messiah!"

Because she was almost deaf, Anna spoke too loud; unbelievers heard what she said and snickered. But their friends understood and excitedly plied Simeon with questions. He answered as best he could until they rushed away to tell others what they'd heard.

Simeon kept searching the crowd, praying in his heart, but there was no sign of the Messiah. After a while he had to give up the vigil. "I must get back to the shop," he told Anna.

Not wanting her muse disturbed, she nodded, and he left her by the pillar humming to herself.

Several weeks went by. Then early one morning Simeon was awakened by the Holy Spirit and knew he must immediately go to the Temple. Reaching Solomon's Porch just as the broad beams of sunlight streamed down upon the courtyard, his heart pounded in his chest. *I should find Anna,* he thought, but at that moment a young couple was approaching the Temple steps. The young man was holding an infant in one arm and a cage with a pair of birds in the other hand. *They've come to make the sacrifice of purification,* Simeon thought.

The baby was crying, and the young man seemed distressed that the baby cried. His wife smiled and took the child in her arms, speaking soothingly to him. The baby cried less, and was soon quieted.

As he stood watching, Simeon sensed the Holy Spirit's confirmation—*the baby is the Christ!* He moved down the steps to meet them, greeted the couple, then reached for the child. Taking the infant up in his arms, he was struck by the light weight of the little, newborn boy. The soft mouth, the wee nose reminded him of his own children when they were first born, and he marveled that such a babe was God's salvation for humanity. The Holy Spirit filled his lips with praise.

Sovereign Lord, as you have promised,
now dismiss your servant in peace.
For my eyes have seen your salvation,
which you have prepared in the sight of all people,
a light for revelation to the Gentiles
and for glory to your people Israel.

The couple was surprised at his words and, looking at each other, wondered. Then Simeon blessed them both and said to Mary, the baby's mother, "This child is destined to cause the falling and rising of many in Israel and to be a sign that will be spoken against, so that the thoughts of many hearts will be revealed."

Simeon paused, reluctant to pass along the rest of what the Holy Spirit was giving him to say. "And a sword will pierce your own soul, too."

The solemn words left the pair quiet and perturbed. Simeon handed the baby back to his mother.

Coming from behind him, Simeon heard the tapping of Anna's cane and turned to see her hobbling toward them. "Anna, the prophetess," he announced to the couple. "Daughter of Phanuel of the tribe of Asher."

"I am Joseph and this is my wife, Mary."

"What is the baby's name?" Anna asked.

"His name is Jesus," the mother replied.

Without asking, Anna perceived the child to be the Christ. Gazing at the infant, not yet six weeks old, his eyes shut against the light, his fingers curled to form a fist, Anna pressed her old wrinkled face against his cheek and praised God.

Blessing the young couple, tears stained Anna's cheeks. But she did not linger long. As Joseph moved to enter the Temple, Anna kissed Mary and hobbled down the steps.

As soon as he could disengage himself, Simeon followed Anna, but she had such a head start on him he could not catch up with her. When he glimpsed her tapping along the cobblestones, he called after her, "Anna!" But she did not hear him. Abruptly, she turned down a side street, and for the moment he lost her. When he came in sight of her again she was knocking on a door. He tried to get through the crowd but was held back. She delivered the message and headed the other way.

Simeon decided not to try to overtake her but to follow and see where she would go. All morning Anna made the rounds of their friends, knocking on their doors. Several times he overheard her telling them the Messiah had come, and he saw them drop what they were doing and head for the Temple. A shopkeeper begged Anna to sit down, but she was in too much of a hurry. Seeing she was overdoing herself, one woman asked her in for tea, but she declined. *I could use a cup of tea,* Simeon thought. Made from dried wildflowers it was a fragrant brew.

Simeon wiped perspiration from his brow and wondered how Anna could keep up such a pace. *Obviously, she won't rest until she tells everyone in the entire city who's looking for him.* Meeting believers on the street, she stopped them, told them the Messiah had come.

Not everyone who was told went to the Temple. As Simeon passed by those who had heard, some of them wore expressions of puzzlement or skepticism. Shopkeepers resumed their work, too busy to disrupt their business day. Simeon thought to himself, *I wonder if the child is still in the Temple. Perhaps those who seek him will not find him there. Even if they do, I wonder if they will believe that tiny babe is our Christ?*

Anna was knocking on the door of what Simeon thought must be the last believer they knew in Jerusalem. He caught up with her and sat down on the steps to wait for her. *Perhaps now she'll let me take her home.*

Sitting there, Simeon wondered what God would do with him. Having seen the glory of Israel in the face of the child, he was ready to depart this life and had told God so. But having observed Anna's zeal, he felt ashamed.

She was coming down the steps. He looked up. The face he saw might have been the face of an angel for its radiance. The joy of implicit trust was there. "Are you tired?" he asked.

"I haven't thought about it," she answered and, leaning on her cane, asked, "Is there anyone else waiting to hear?"

STUDY QUESTIONS

1. What do you think was the role of a prophetess?
   A. She was a spokeswoman for God just as a male prophet was.

B. In the tradition of Miriam, Deborah, and Huldah some prophetesses were musicians, others counselors, and some made predictions.

C. I think her role was to help others through difficult times by listening and counseling.

2. There was corruption in the Temple. What influence do you think Anna had on people who worshiped there?

A. Since there were people in Jerusalem expecting the Messiah, perhaps she led some of them into that knowledge.

B. An old lady like that would've been outspoken in letting the money-changers and proud officials know that they were sinning.

C. Since she was in the Women's Court day and night she was available at all hours for prostitutes and other outcasts who would feel more comfortable coming at night.

3. Anna fasted as well as prayed. Did she set an example for us today?

A. Not necessarily. Even in the history of Israel God ordered only one fast day and many feasts.

B. Since not only Anna but Jesus fasted there must be value and purpose in it.

C. Jesus gave instructions about fasting and said those who fast will be rewarded (Matt. 6:16).

Something to Ponder: How does a young woman get to be the kind of woman Anna was?

10

The Centurion

I TELL YOU, I HAVE NOT FOUND SUCH GREAT FAITH EVEN IN
ISRAEL.

Scripture: John 4:46–54; Mark 1:21–28,
40–45; 2:1–12; Matt. 8:5–13; Luke 7:1–10

Junius had been in the army sixteen years, the last six
stationed in Capernaum. He had come a long way from
the village where he was born at the foot of the Italian Alps.
A plebeian, he had joined the army in order to have Roman
citizenship, but now as he looked back upon it, citizenship
seemed unimportant compared with his spiritual concerns.

Within Junius's legion there were six thousand men di-
vided into ten cohorts, each of which had three *maniples*
consisting of either sixty or one hundred twenty men. Each
maniple had centurions leading a hundred men each. Junius
was a centurion, and beneath him in rank were the *principales,*
noncommissioned officers detailed for special duty. Such was
his friend and servant Benaiah, a Jew from Capernaum.

The two men had been through many trials together.
Once in a skirmish with brigands, Junius had been wounded,
and Benaiah tended his wounds and nursed him back to
health. Then there were the challenges of drilling young
recruits; inspecting their arms, food, and clothing; making
ruffians into Roman soldiers of distinction. He could not have
done it without the faithful Benaiah.

Now separated from his legion for duty in Capernaum,
Junius was even more dependent on Benaiah, for his knowledge of Jewish ways and thought gave Junius the insight he

needed to deal with the problems in Galilee. Through it all the two men had grown to respect and love each other.

Benaiah was religious, but he was unlike the pompous religious Jews Junius had seen in Jerusalem. There was truth in the man and a passion for duty such as he had never witnessed in any other soldier. It aroused the centurion's curiosity, and he pursued his interest by going to the old synagogue by the fountain where Benaiah worshiped. There he heard a plea for funds to build another synagogue on the other side of town. Benaiah said the Jews were poor, and their plea seemed hopeless.

Junius studied the matter. In his knapsack was a sack of silver, plunder he had taken years before in the ruins of an old town. In addition, he knew officials who would appropriate funds to win Roman favor with the Jews. *Perhaps Jews can have their synagogue after all. At least it's worth a try.*

And so the synagogue was built, much to the delight of the Jews, who praised him profusely. Lest Junius grow proud, his servant cautioned him, "Sir, it is not by works we gain our soul's salvation."

"Then, pray tell, what is it?"

"Salvation is of the Jews."

"I believe that. Explain it to me."

But the servant could not. "I only know, sir, that when the Messiah comes he will bring salvation."

Junius did not press him for details. Benaiah was old and did not feel well most of the time. Besides, they had discussed the matter many times with no satisfactory conclusions.

It was not until a Nazarene carpenter began preaching and teaching in Galilee that Junius's interest in Jewish thought intensified. Galileans, returning from feasts in Jerusalem, had brought back tall tales about the man, Jesus, but the centurion did not concern himself with hearsay. It was told him that even Samaritans were flocking after the Nazarene! Yet he heard this carpenter, this rabbi, was not deceived by his popularity. Someone said Jesus told the Galileans that, like prophets before him, he would not have honor in his own country. The statement expressed a realism Junius admired; yet it puzzled him that a carpenter created such a stir, and he took it upon himself to study the Nazarene to find out all he could about him.

One day in the line of duty Junius was called to the home of a royal official in Capernaum, a man of no mean reputation in the service of Herod Antipas. When their business was completed, Junius asked about the official's son who had been ill with pox.

"Haven't you heard?" the man asked. "Jesus healed my boy."

"Healed him?"

"Yes! And without so much as laying a hand on him." He was anxious to tell the story. They sat down on the terrace. "I heard that Jesus was in Cana—perhaps you remember, last year at a wedding there, Jesus turned water to wine."

Junius nodded.

"Well, my son was at death's door, as you well know. In my desperation I decided to go to Jesus. When I found him, I begged him to come to my home. At first I thought he was scolding me because he said, 'Unless you people see miraculous signs and wonders you will never believe.' Well, I didn't argue with him. I had no one else to turn to, and nothing he could say would keep me from imploring him to help my son. I said, 'Sir, come down before my child dies.' "

"Did he go?"

"No. He told me I could go home, that my son would live."

"And you went home?"

"Yes, I left Cana right away. The next day as I was coming down the lane to my house, my servants came running to meet me. I could tell by their beaming faces that something had happened. When they told me my son was well—you can imagine my relief and joy. I asked the servants when the boy began to improve. They told me the fever left him the day before at the seventh hour—the exact same time Jesus spoke those words to me!"

It was an amazing story, and Junius asked his friend to repeat it and reiterate every detail as he sought to understand just what happened and what it was about the Nazarene that gave him such results.

There were other miracles performed by Jesus in Capernaum, and when one Sabbath evening it was rumored that Jesus might be asked to teach, Junius went to the synagogue to hear him. He along with others in the congregation were astonished at the way Jesus taught. Unlike other teachers, he never quoted a rabbi or scribe to support what he had to say. *He speaks with authority,* Junius concluded, *independent of what other people may think.*

While Junius was in the synagogue that day, a man possessed by an evil spirit disrupted the service, crying out, "What do you want with us, Jesus of Nazareth? Have you come to destroy us? I know who you are—the Holy One of God!"

Jesus rebuked the spirit. "Be quiet!" he commanded. "Come out of him!" Immediately the man fell to the ground, shaking violently, and the spirit left him, shrieking!

Everybody was amazed. Benaiah voiced what others were saying, "What is this? A new teaching—and with authority! He even gives orders to evil spirits, and they obey him." The servant was wide-eyed, and Junius shook his head, finding it hard to believe what he had seen and heard.

After that day there were reports of many other healings, with people coming from miles around, bringing their sick. Junius pitied the Nazarene, stampeded as he was with urgent pleas, and thought it wise when Jesus left Capernaum to preach in other Galilean towns.

Going about his duties, Junius often thought about these events. Never had he known such a man who not only spoke with authority but exercised authority over all manner of illness and even the spirit world. *Therein lies his difference,*

Junius perceived. *In himself he has authority to say what he says and to do what he does.*

When Junius expressed himself to Benaiah, his servant was too ill to respond. He looked in the dear old man's face, ashen from the pain, his eyes bright with fever, and Junius worried that he might die.

"It is only a crisis," the medical officer told the centurion. "He'll come around this time."

Junius left Benaiah heavy of heart. He decided to go down to the synagogue. As he walked along the street, he gave no notice to a man shouting excitedly. But the fellow ran after him. "Sir, don't you remember me?"

Junius frowned.

"I am the leper you always gave alms to."

"You're no leper."

"I've been healed! Jesus healed me!"

Junius looked at him long and hard. "Yes, I do believe you have," he replied, then turned to go on his way. A thought occurred to him, and he turned back. "Where is Jesus now?"

"On the other side of town—in a house. There's quite a mob, I hear. They had a stretcher case, and when they couldn't get the sick man inside where Jesus was, they tore up the roof and lowered the man down. Can you believe that! Desperate—those who are suffering are absolutely desperate. If he touches them, they're made well."

It isn't in his touch, Junius thought. *He has only to say the word,* and he continued down the street. *I won't bother him,* he decided.

In the months that followed, Benaiah would rally, then regress. Little by little he was wasting away, his limbs paralyzed, his suffering excruciating. Junius knew he did not have long to live, and he felt so desperate he expressed his concern to the Jewish elders. "What would you think of asking Jesus to heal my servant?"

They agreed. "Since the rabbi is a Jew, we'll send members of the congregation to him to ask." And so they sent a delegation.

As they walked, the emissaries discussed what approach, what appeal they might use. An elder expressed himself. "Since we of Israel are God's chosen people and all the world is to be blessed through us, we must tell the Nazarene the good the centurion has done for our nation."

"How he favors us—how he built the synagogue for us," another added.

"Yes, that's the kind of thing."

They found Jesus in the house where he was staying and began earnestly beseeching him. "This man deserves to have you do this because he loves our nation and has built our synagogue."

Jesus stood up to go with them. "I will come and heal him," he said.

Some of the Jews ran ahead to tell Junius. When they reached his house and told the centurion Jesus was on his way, he asked them, "What did you say to him?"

And when they told him, Junius was upset. "You told him I am *worthy?* that he should heal Benaiah because I am *worthy?*"

He turned aside to friends. "Please, go," he said. "Tell Jesus, 'Lord, don't trouble yourself, for I do not deserve to have you come under my roof. That is why I did not even consider myself worthy to come to you. But say the word, and my servant will be healed." He hesitated, then added in a low voice, "For I myself am a man under authority, with soldiers under me. I tell this one, 'Go,' and he goes and that one, 'Come,' and he comes. I say to my servant, 'Do this,' and he does it."

After they were gone, Junius sat down beside Benaiah's bed and took the old man's hand. In a few minutes Jesus would speak the word, and Benaiah would be well. It was a moment Junius did not want to miss.

An officer pried open the sick man's lips, helping a servant force a reed between his teeth. For some time they tried to coax Benaiah to take the wine, but there was no response. "I'm sorry, sir," the officer said to Junius, "he hasn't the strength to drink. Shall we bother to bathe him, sir? Perhaps he's suffered enough—we should let him go."

"Bathe him," Junius ordered defiantly, and the servant went to fetch the water.

The minutes dragged by as he waited for the word that would release his friend from pain, loose his limbs from paralysis. Junius spoke soothingly to the dying man. "It won't be long, dear Benaiah. The Lord will soon hear and give the word."

With a basin of warm water and a towel, the manservant knelt down to bathe Benaiah. Wiping the dry mouth and nose, the eyes and forehead, Junius heard a faint sigh escape the sick man's lips. "Don't worry, old friend. Soon you'll be up and on your feet."

They were nearly done with the bath when Benaiah opened his eyes, looked around as if coming awake after a long sleep. "Sir," he said. "What's happening?"

The servant fell back astonished.

Junius smiled and waited for the full realization to flood his friend's sensibilities. Benaiah slowly raised his head, propped himself up on his elbows. "I want to get up," he said in a strong voice.

The servant's eyes seemed to be popping out of his head.

"Of course, you can!" Junius told him, and to the servant, "Get his clothes!"

Benaiah stood on his feet, and the two men embraced. "Jesus healed you," Junius told him.

About that time the friends who had carried the message to Jesus returned. They stared at Benaiah in astonishment. "Did you tell Jesus what I said?" Junius asked.

"We did."

"What did he say?"

"He told the crowd following him, 'I tell you the truth, I have not found anyone in Israel with such great faith.' "

Junius was overwhelmed. "He said that?"

"He said more than that. It seems he thinks Gentiles like you will join the ranks of Israel in the kingdom of heaven."

"What did he say?"

"He said, 'I say to you that many will come from the east and the west and will take their places at the feast with Abraham, Isaac, and Jacob in the kingdom of heaven.' "

Junius bowed his head and closed his eyes. Gratitude welled up inside him—so much so he could scarce contain the fountain of tears threatening him. Benaiah put his arm around his shoulder. "Sir, I'm really quite well now. What would you have me do?"

STUDY QUESTIONS

1. Do you think the "fictionized" background of this centurion is valid?
   A. The military details seem historically correct and his reasons for being in the army are believable.
   B. The author could have added the suggestion that the centurion had read the Old Testament in Greek which generated faith.
   C. Since he was stationed in Galilee, a small part of the country, it is reasonable to assume that he had heard about Jesus' works in that area and may have heard him speak in the synagogue.

2. What do you think the centurion meant by comparing his authority with the authority of Jesus?
   A. Whereas religious Jews emphasized keeping the Law rather than exercising faith, the centurion understood that faith in the authority of Jesus was what mattered.

B. The centurion was saying that the command of Christ, rather than his touch or presence, would heal his servant.

C. He was impressed with the authority of Jesus over illness and evil spirits, and rather than just say, "Speak the word," he wanted to emphasize the authority back of that word.

3. Is there anything today that corresponds to the Jews' appealing to Jesus on the ground that the centurion was deserving?

A. When bad things happen to good people we sometimes hear the complaint that they deserved better treatment from God.

B. The Jewish messengers sounded like the Lord was there to do their bidding rather than the other way around. That attitude is prevalent today.

C. Sometimes in choosing church officers people are chosen because they are financially successful, as if that qualifies them for leadership.

Something to Ponder: When Jesus was on earth he was in only one place at a time yet his word was effective some distance away. How much more accessible is Jesus today—no longer limited by his body to one place but universally present, instantly available.

11

The Syrophoenician Woman

WOMAN, YOU HAVE GREAT FAITH!

Scripture: Matt. 15:21–28; Mark 7:24–30

As a woman of Canaanite descent and of the Greek religion, I had no interest in Jewish people or their views. My gods had served me well, and I wanted no part of any narrow-minded culture such as the Jews' legalistic religion imposed. They were an arrogant lot who treated Gentiles as if they were untouchable—calling us dogs and other derogatory names.

My husband once took me to Jerusalem when he was going there on business, and what I saw of the Jews' Temple and their ritual was far inferior to the temples in Tyre or, for that matter, the temples of Sidon. My husband said they believed a Jewish Messiah would come and restore the kingdom to Israel. "They expect another King David—a descendant of David." We laughed at that.

But then my husband died, and my child became ill. The priests of Tyre could not exorcise the demon that plagued my poor little Demeter, so I went to a sorceress who gave me a potion in a jar, telling me to give it to the child before the demon came upon her. But as I was leaving, I looked over my shoulder, and the sorceress was laughing at me.

Even so, I tried the potion, and for a while it seemed to work, but then it failed. My daughter was worse than ever. Old women gave me nostrums they vowed would drive out demons, and I tried them all, but nothing helped. It pains me now to think of the way, time and time again, Demeter was flung about the room as the demon tried to kill her. Her body bore bruises and cuts from those bouts. I could never leave her alone. Whenever the demon willed, it could send her into a trance or a convulsion. There were nights when she did not sleep but lay whimpering, afraid and tormented.

I had given up hope when I began hearing about a man from Nazareth who could perform miracles. That did not raise my hopes, but I did inquire of travelers who had seen him, heard him teach. I listened to all their stories, well aware of how stories tend to be exaggerated in the telling. Yet when they spoke of him they sometimes called him the "son of David," and I recalled what my husband had told me about the Jewish Messiah. I held that thought in reserve, wondering if there could be any truth in what I had heard and if the rabbi might be the promised one.

Then one day a peddler was attracting a lot of attention by recounting one miracle after another he swore he saw Jesus perform—lepers healed, blind people made to see, and, yes, demons cast out. I did not believe all he said, but I had heard enough to know Jesus could help Demeter. Whether or not the Jews believed he was their Messiah, I believed he could be mine.

Getting to Jesus posed several problems. For one thing, I did not know how I could find him. You see, I could not take Demeter anywhere, and I could not arrange to leave her for any length of time. There was also the matter of my being a Syrophoenician, a Gentile. By nature I am a timid woman, and knowing how the Jews rebuff people like me, I would not have dared approach the rabbi except for one casual remark the peddler made. The comment kept coming back to me. "He loves children," the peddler said. "It doesn't matter who they are, he takes them up in his arms, blesses them. He never passes by a child."

If he loves children, I reasoned, *he will help my child*. I determined that I would find this Jesus, and in my heart I prayed. I began asking people where he might be found. A coppersmith recently returned from Caesarea told me he heard Jesus had left Galilee and was heading north. It was too good to be true. "If that is true, he should be in this region in three days," the man said.

Is this the answer to my prayer, I asked myself.

The main road is within walking distance of my house. So, leaving Demeter in the care of a neighbor, I left before daybreak to sit by the road in case he came. I worried that I would not recognize him, so I questioned every passerby. For three days I waited but to no avail.

Then a woman who seemed to know what she was talking about told me the Nazarene would never take the main road, that he did everything possible to avoid crowds. I was at a loss to know what more I could do. My heart as heavy as lead, I headed home. I must confess, as I walked down that rutted road, I could no longer fight back the tears. How could I face another day with my tortured child ranting and raving, screaming night and day.

As I rounded the curve close by my home, I saw a company of men coming toward me. They seemed deep in conversation, attentive to one man in the midst of them. I was reluctant to interrupt them, but I had to ask. A dark, handsome man disregarded my approach so that I had to step aside to let him pass. "Sir," I said, "I am looking for Jesus of Nazareth. He's supposed to be in this region—"

He pointed toward the man in the company whom the others were intent upon listening to. My heart was in my throat, my tongue was tied. The men were striding forward, heading for a house. I ran after them. "Lord, Son of David, have mercy on me! My daughter is suffering terribly from demon possession."

I followed them inside the courtyard imploring the rabbi

again and again, but he ignored me. Proud as I am, I was too desperate to be put off by insult.

His friends scowled at me, annoyed by my persistence. "Send her away," they told him, "for she keeps crying out after us."

Jesus' answer stabbed me through and through. "I was sent only to the lost sheep of the house of Israel," he said.

I fell down at his feet. "Lord, help me!"

He looked down at me and said, "First let the children eat all they want, for it is not right to take the children's bread and toss it to their dogs."

I would not give up. I could not. Try to understand, if you can—my child was *demon-possessed!* "Yes, Lord," I said, "but even the dogs under the table eat the children's crumbs."

"Woman," he said, "you have great faith! Your request is granted."

I cannot tell you how I felt. It was as if one wave after another swept over me—such joy I cannot describe. I would have kissed his feet, but his friends were standing between us, preventing me.

I ran out of the house and down the road as fast as I could. The neighbor was standing in the door, her eyes as wide as two moons, bursting to tell me what I already knew. I ran past her, and there was Demeter lying on the bed, as calm and beautiful as a little flower. I took her in my arms and hugged her to my breast, her little face soft against my cheek. "Don't cry," she said. "Everything's all right now. The demon's all gone."

Brushing back her hair, I wept. "And, Darling, he'll never, never return."

STUDY QUESTIONS

1. What do you think of films about demon possession?
   A. I don't think we should advertise the works of the devil.

    B. If they scare people enough perhaps they won't dabble in the occult.

    C. Impressionable minds can be influenced adversely.

2. Do you think there is demon possession in civilized countries?

    A. Atrocities are certainly inspired of the devil. The perpetrators might very well be demon possessed.

    B. Satan worshipers are undoubtedly possessed by demons when they commit heineous crimes.

    C. Demon possession might be misdiagnosed as mental illness.

3. How do we measure "great faith"?

    A. To me great faith is when you don't get what you want and you hang in there.

    B. Faith as a grain of mustard seed is enough if it's placed in God.

    C. Great faith is simple trust and total reliance on God.

Something to Ponder: In Jesus' day the Jews looked down on Gentiles. Since then, in some circles, the tables have been reversed; today there is antisemitism. One of the blessings of heaven will be the eradication of discrimination. That much of heaven we should have now in the body of Christ.

12

Mary

IT WAS MEANT THAT SHE SHOULD SAVE THIS PERFUME FOR
THE DAY OF MY BURIAL.

Scripture: John 11:55–12:11; Matt. 26:6–13; Mark 14:3–9

Pilgrims thronged the streets of Jerusalem as Mary and
Martha left the Temple to return to Bethany. They had
come as the pilgrims had, to purify themselves for the coming
Passover. Mary was disturbed by what she had heard in the
Temple. The courtyard was rife with talk of Lazarus being
raised from the dead, and people everywhere were discussing
Jesus. She overheard several Pharisees, their heads close together, talking, and one of them said, "We need to do away
with him."

"The sooner the better," another agreed.

They can only mean Lazarus, she thought. *Oh, how could
they?*

One of them asked the others, "Do you think Jesus will
come to Passover?"

"If he knows what's good for him, he won't."

Oh, dear, Mary worried. *He will come to the feast, I know
he will. They'll kill him, too.*

Hurrying to avoid being recognized, the sisters slipped
down an alley. Martha was leading the way past some sheep
pens. A shepherd's wife, holding a lamb in her arms, eyed
them curiously. Martha asked the price. The woman smiled.
She recognizes us, Mary thought, and her first impulse was to
turn and slip away as fast as she could, but the woman took
Martha by the arm, put down the lamb and led the two of

them aside. Cautiously looking about, she spoke in a whisper. "I know you. You are the sisters of Lazarus, who is raised from the dead." Nervously she glanced over her shoulder. "Remember me? My father's house was just down the road from yours. Of course, we were poor and unlearned. You are friends of Jesus."

"Yes," Martha acknowledged. "I remember seeing you at the well in Bethany. Your name escapes me—"

"I am Adiel, daughter of Hamutal." Looking furtively about she drew them closer. "I must warn you—the chief priests, Annas himself, and most of the Pharisees have given out the word that if anyone knows where Jesus is they must tell them so they can arrest him."

"Yes, we know," Martha said. "We heard the same from others in the Temple."

"Is it true that you are honoring him at a supper?"

"Aye, it is true. On this Sabbath eve. Come if you can."

"I will. I will indeed," the woman answered. "Lazarus will be there?"

"Of course. We'll all be there."

The woman fidgeted, wanting to say more.

"What is it?" Martha asked.

"It's not for me to say."

Mary tugged at Martha's arm for Mary knew what the woman wished to tell them. "I think we'd better go." *I don't want Martha to hear anything about the religious leaders' talk of killing Lazarus,* she said to herself.

"What about the lamb?" Martha asked.

"There's plenty of time to find a lamb," Mary told her. You have six days before Passover."

On the way home, Martha worried. "Do you think they will try to kill our brother again?"

"I daresay they would if they could." Mary sounded brave, but the threat so frightened her she could not talk about it.

"Why are you walking so fast?" Martha complained. "Everything's ready for the meal. All we have to do is serve the guests."

"I want to be there when Jesus comes."

"They'll be a while yet. I only hope the house of Simon the Leper is large enough to take care of all the people who'll come. I'm making sure we'll have enough food and that it is properly prepared. I'd never serve a meal Simon prepared."

The women arrived home none too soon. The courtyard was full of people milling about, anxious to glimpse Lazarus—waiting for Jesus to come. Already the servants were washing the feet of Thaddeus and Nathanael, who reached Bethany ahead of the other disciples. Mary greeted them, then made her way inside the house.

The women busied themselves with the final preparations of the meal. "Mary, would you please get me the salt?" Martha asked, and Mary went to a shelf where they kept jars of apothecary herbs and ointments. Looking for the salt, she discovered an old alabaster bottle hidden in the corner. It was a vial of spikenard she had almost forgotten.

"What's that you're looking at?" Martha asked.

"That jar of nard."

"Oh, yes, the only ointment we didn't use when we buried Lazarus."

"About a pint, I'd say."

"Be careful, Mary. That's very expensive." She stopped what she was doing and came over to examine the alabaster vial. "I remember the day Papa bought the resin from an old trader. A stranger to our country, he had been traveling for a very long time . . . said he came from the East. You were too young to remember, but the old man sat in the courtyard that afternoon and told us all about the spikenard plant. He said it only grows high in the mountains, so high the air is thin and only mountaineers can risk the climb.

"Papa paid as much for this perfume as some people earn

in a year's time. He could well afford it, and he was not content until he had accumulated enough of the ointment to bury all of us." She turned away, a sadness coming over her. "We've had so many burials—I wonder who will be next."

Mary touched her sister's arm. "Think only of the joy that is ours—our brother was dead, and now he is alive."

"I do, Mary. I do."

Mary, holding the vial up to the light, tried to see what was inside but couldn't.

"You can't see through alabaster," Martha said. "Besides, there's nothing to see. The way they process the nard reduces it to a powder; then it's mixed with oil. Please, Mary, do be careful."

Mary set the vial back on the shelf. For a moment she lingered, studying the beautiful jar, and in her heart she prayed, *Oh, Lord, may we not have to use it to bury Lazarus again.*

Voices in the courtyard were growing louder, and when Mary looked outside there were people all along the road leading to the house, curious neighbors and friends waiting for Jesus. "Martha, where's Lazarus?" Mary asked.

"He's waiting for us at Simon's."

Nathanael came looking for Mary and beckoned her to follow him. Finding a quiet corner, they sat down.

"What is it, Nathanael?"

"There is something troubling me, Mary." His long, lean face was drawn. "It's about Jesus. When we were on our way here, he started talking about dying. It's not the first time . . . remember, I told you before. Of course, I don't see how that could be . . . what with his power and all. But it is unsettling. Judas says it'll never happen—that a man who says he is our king will not die before he reigns."

Mary gave little heed to anything Judas Iscariot said. The

man made her feel uncomfortable, what with his good looks and smart ways.

Thaddeus and Martha joined them. Mary looked up at Nathanael. "What exactly did Jesus say?"

"Well, essentially he said he'd be turned over to the Gentiles and mistreated, then he'd be killed."

Mary felt her blood run cold. "Anything more?"

"Not that I remember."

Thaddeus spoke up, "He said something about the third day he would rise again."

Martha reminded them, "He is the Resurrection."

Mary agreed. "Thaddeus, you heard what Jesus said; what do you make of it?"

"Mary, there's nothing to worry about. You saw how Jesus acted at your brother's tomb. Remember the antagonism he showed toward death? Remember how angry he was? Feeling as he does about death and with all the power he has, do you think he would let someone kill him? No, that will never happen. Judas says—"

She didn't want to hear what Judas said. *Jesus said he will die. Die he will.*

Shouts were going up from the roadway. "It's the Lord!" Mary exclaimed and rushed out to meet him.

Peter stopped her. "Mary, how will you feed such a crowd?"

"We've hired a public house. You're all to go to Simon's place," she told him, hurrying toward Jesus.

The word spread, and the entourage made its way up the road to Simon's public house. Only since Jesus had cured him of leprosy did the old man operate the inn. Lazarus stood in the doorway with Simon welcoming the guests.

How the people marveled at Lazarus, at first too awed to speak and then assailing him with a flood of questions. Laughing, he begged off. "Friends, I am alive and well. What more can I tell you?"

"What was it like being dead?" a small boy asked.

Lazarus stooped down, laid his hands on the boy's shoulders, and looked him in the eye. "I really can't say."

The boy was satisfied, but the grownups were not. Simon interrupted their rush of questions.

"Come, let's eat," he told them. Hungry as they were, the guests were willing to forego answers in preference for food. Like sheep going into the fold, they streamed through the doorway.

Mary could not enter into festivities at the table because her heart was anxious for both her brother and her Lord. Drawing apart, she went outside and sat in the courtyard as if watching the sun setting in the west. *I believe him,* she said to herself. *They are going to kill Jesus.* Tears welled up in her eyes. And then Martha's words came to her: *He is the Resurrection.* The words came with such clarity she understood in an instant. He had said, *"On the third day I will rise."* Of course, *he will rise!*

The realization made Mary alternately grieved and then at peace. *He must die, but he will rise,* she repeated to herself. *What can I do? Is there anything I can do for him?* In a few minutes she remembered the spikenard and jumping up, she ran down the path that cut through the vineyard to home.

By the time Mary returned to the inn, the guests were busy eating, talking as they ate, laughing. She slipped in quietly so that no one noticed her. Fortunately, she entered near the place where Jesus reclined at a table, otherwise she would have had difficulty getting through the crowd that jammed the place. Only Judas noticed her as she bent down and broke the seal on the alabaster. He stopped eating and stared at her as she raised the vial above Jesus' head and poured a stream of oil on his hair. A rivulet ran down onto his beard, forming droplets that hung suspended.

The pungent scent began to be noticed, and people paused to see what she was about. Pouring the oil into her palm, Mary lathered it on the Lord's bare foot; she poured another palmful and used that on the other foot. The oil ran down between his toes onto the floor as its fragrance filled the air. A murmur went through the room. Mary let down her hair and, dabbing the Lord's feet with it, soaked up the excess oil.

When she held up the vial there was yet some oil, and as she was about to pour the remainder on Jesus' head, Judas grabbed her arm. His dark eyes smoldered. "Why wasn't this perfume sold and the money given to the poor? It was worth a year's wages."

Others in the room agreed with him.

"Leave her alone," Jesus answered. "It was meant that she should save this perfume for the day of my burial. She has done a beautiful thing to me. The poor you will always have with you, but you will not always have me."

Judas withdrew his hand and backed away. Mary finished pouring the oil on Jesus' head, then slipped away to help Martha.

Jesus looked around the table. "When she poured this perfume on my body, she did it to prepare me for burial. I tell you the truth, wherever this gospel is preached throughout the world, what she has done will also be told, in memory of her."

During the days that followed, Mary did not share the anxiety of Mary Magdalene, Salome, Joanna, and the other women. She knew it was inevitable that Jesus would die as he had said. And after he was crucified she did not grieve as they did.

When the Sabbath was ended and the women went to the tomb with more burial spices, Mary did not go with them—her ministrations had been done. Instead, she waited expectantly. The third day had dawned.

STUDY QUESTIONS

1. Can you think of other expensive gifts given to God such as Mary offered?
   - A. The wise men gave gold, frankincense, and myrrh to the Baby Jesus.
   - B. The Israelites gave so much material for the building of the tabernacle that Moses told them to stop. Tons of gold and silver were given by David and Solomon for the building of the Temple.
   - C. Relatively speaking, the widow's mite was costly because it was all the woman had. Jesus said she gave *more* than people who gave much out of their abundance.

2. Is there a temptation in our expenditure of money today to think as Judas did?
   - A. Let a church board appropriate money for an expensive item to be used in worship and invariably someone will criticize them for not spending it on the poor or for more practical purposes.
   - B. A stingy or selfish marriage partner might criticize a mate for spending too much time or money in the Lord's work.
   - C. God loves a cheerful giver and when someone gives grudgingly he or she isn't giving for the right reasons.

3. In what way is Mary's story unique?
   - A. She was apparently the only person who truly believed Jesus when he said he was going to die.
   - B. She's the only person in the Bible to whom Jesus said, "She has done a beautiful thing to me."
   - C. Jesus said that wherever the gospel is preached what Mary did would be told in memory of her.

Something to Ponder: Although our stories will not be written in the Bible as Mary's was, isn't it possible that we might do something "beautiful" for Jesus today that will be remembered forever?

13

Paul

ABOUT MIDNIGHT PAUL AND SILAS WERE PRAYING AND
SINGING HYMNS TO GOD.

Scripture: Acts 16

P aul and his companions would not have ventured into
Macedonia except for the vision. They had fully intended to go into Bithynia but were constrained by the Spirit
of Christ. Then at Troas a "man of Macedonia" appeared to
Paul, beseeching him to cross over the Aegean Sea and help
the people there. Obediently, the apostle, with Silas, Timothy, and Luke, found the first ship available and bought passage to the district of Macedonia.

As the missionaries sat on the deck of the cargo ship, her
sails full blown by the steady breeze and white against the
blue sky, Luke told them about his hometown, Philippi.
"That's where I studied medicine," he said. "The school is
connected with a guild of physicians, and some of the most
learned practitioners of the medical arts teach there."

Paul knew it was providential that Luke had come to his
aid in Troas. Suffering from a malady that of late had become
increasingly vexing, Paul found relief after Luke adminis-
tered certain medicines. A learned man, Luke was not limited
to medical knowledge but was a student of history as well.

"My grandfather," Luke said, "a native son, remembered
the battle of Actium just outside Philippi. I know you're
familiar with that one—Octavius and Antony defeated
Brutus and Cassius."

The three acknowledged that they did know about Actium.

"The victory gave them control of the Via Egnatia, the

road that connects Rome with Asia. When the battle was over, Octavius had to do something with the legions of soldiers under his command, so he decided to make Philippi a Roman colony where the soldiers could settle and make a life for themselves. He was known as Octavius then, but you know his name changed to Augustus when he became emperor.

"The Romans gave us good public works and roads," he conceded, "but we Greeks taught them how to read and write."

The wash from the prow showered Paul with salt spray, but he did not move to avoid it. The spray felt good on his face. "Does Philippi have a synagogue?" he asked.

"No, not inside the city. The Romans allow all kinds of religions—many of the Greek gods are worshiped there—the god Liber Pater from Thrace, the goddess Bendis, the goddess Athena." He was counting them off on his long slim fingers. "Even the Egyptian Isis, the Anatolian Cybele. And, of course the Romans brought their Jupiter and Mars and emperor cult." The dark brown eyes saddened; his voice dropped. "My family holds fast to the Greek gods."

Paul knew it had not been easy for Luke to break with his family and heritage when he put his faith in Christ. But once Luke applied that analytical mind to the Scriptures and the Holy Spirit convinced him of the truth, he forthrightly committed himself.

"My father is Greek," Timothy said, his young voice sympathetic.

"All those religions but no synagogue?" Silas asked.

"Not inside the city. You see, you Jews teach that there is only one God. Such a religion is a threat to the many gods worshiped in Philippi; they won't tolerate faith in one invisible God. There's no synagogue in the city nor outside the wall for some distance."

Silas looked puzzled. "What do you mean 'outside the wall'?"

"There is an area beyond the wall where no burial or foreign cult is permitted. The boundary is marked by the colonial arch over the Via Egnatia. Beyond the arch there may be a synagogue down near the river. I know a woman named Euodia goes to pray there on Jewish Sabbath days."

"Which river is that?" Timothy asked.

"The Ganga or Gangites, as some people call it. It's just beyond the arch, about a mile from the heart of town."

"That's the river where Alexander defeated the Persians, isn't it?"

Luke looked pleased that Timothy knew that. "Your father must be a good teacher," he said, "for you are quite right; perhaps you'll see the battlefield. Alexander gave our city its name. Philippi is named for his father, Philip."

After a few days, the ship docked at the port city of Neapolis in the Roman province of Macedonia. The men disembarked to walk the ten miles to Philippi on the famous Via Egnatia. As they hiked along the road they were passed by cavalrymen and traders, farmers and officials going to and from the city, some journeying from faraway places. Dressed in foreign attire, many of the travelers were obviously from distant lands, while others were thoroughly Grecian in dress and manner. Luke and Timothy in their short, lightweight tunics looked like natives, while Paul and Silas with their thick beards and Palestinian cloaks looked distinctly foreign.

Paul did not find Macedonia strange. His own native city of Tarsus was a free city, much like what he expected to find in Philippi, a crossroads between East and West. Nor would Silas find Philippi totally strange, Paul thought, since Silas was a Roman citizen himself, had lived in the cosmopolitan cities of Jerusalem and Antioch, and had now traveled through Asia Minor.

Paul himself had the civic rights of both Tarsus and Rome. His father had distinguished himself as a soldier in combat and was rewarded with Roman citizenship, which was automatically passed on to his son. Not only did citizenship give Paul the right to vote, it gave him the protection of

Rome. He could not be bound or punished without a trial or ever subjected to flogging, a favorite means of wringing a confession of wrongdoing from a victim.

As Paul remembered Lystra and the stoning he received there, he took small comfort in the fact of his citizenship. *There is no protection from a mob,* he told himself.

As they drew nearer Philippi, a mountain to the west made for a beautiful view. "That's Mount Pangaeus," Luke told them. "There are gold and silver mines up there."

The city was pleasantly situated, surrounded on three sides by mountains. Although not the capital of the district, Paul knew Philippi was a rival to Amphipolis and outclassed it as a leader in the Macedonian district.

Luke stopped in the road and, pointing, said, "See that hill over there? It's a spur of the Orbelos, and that's where the acropolis stands. See, the city lies at the foot of it."

A mist hovered over the city, huddled as it was around the base of the hill.

As they moved on, Paul wondered what kind of reception they would receive in Philippi. Except for the vision, there was little to suggest a welcome.

"I wish I could invite you to stay with my relatives," Luke said. "But that would not be wise."

Paul was quick to reassure him. "Don't apologize, Luke. We'd rather stay at our own expense than take from those who don't acknowledge Christ. In that way our motives can't be misunderstood."

"We have enough between us," Silas said, "for lodging and for meals."

As they looked for a public house, they walked past a theater where actors were rehearsing a drama. Beyond the theater were the public baths and colonnades. The pools looked inviting. Paul could think of nothing he would enjoy more than to submerge himself in the cool water and wash away the dust and grime of the road. Luke must have noted the wistful look in his eye because he said, "There are fountains up ahead. We'll stop there for a drink."

To get to the fountains they had to pass through the marketplace. Unlike marketplaces in his homeland, Paul noted the elegance of the buildings closing in the square where the market was held. The stone pavement of the square was adorned with Greek sculpture. People, dogs, goats, asses, oxen congregated there with speakers holding court, women socializing, and children chasing each other. The aisles between the makeshift stands were clogged with bargain hunters, half-drunk youths, and filthy perverts.

Luke and Timothy led the way through a covered arcade where shops of leathergoods, sweetmeats, fish, cloth, reading materials, utensils, and the like were on either side. The smell of onions and peppers was lost among the odors of perspiration, the smoke of burning fat, and the animal dung. A ragged beggar, blind and crippled, cried out for help. Timothy bought bread and gave it to him. Luke bargained for fruit, and Paul found cheese at a good price. Silas caught up with them. "Here, I bought some smoked fish."

As the four walked along eating, dogs trotted behind them, scavengers of every scrap they dropped. Passing by a knot of women crowded around a black-robed girl telling fortunes, they heard someone demand of her, "Tell me who robbed my hen nest of setting eggs."

The men continued on along the concourse where craft makers in gold and silver, blacksmiths, and metal workers plied their trades. Moneylenders and priests, military officers and minstrels made themselves available there. A group of idlers was watching gamblers roll their dice.

Emerging from the arcade, Paul remarked, "It's good to breathe fresh air again," and the others agreed. As they walked down the street they spoke admiringly of the handsome public buildings, the library, and the monuments to Roman heroes. But from a dark alley a harlot beckoned to them. Ignoring her they soon reached the porticoes where the fountains graced the facades of two temples. Spouts of water lept and fell, spraying crystal droplets sparkling in the sun.

After the apostles drank their fill, they splashed water on

their faces, necks, and arms. As Paul washed himself he felt an eagerness to preach the gospel there. *These Philippians pride themselves on being a free city,* he thought to himself. *How little do they realize that the god of this world has taken them captive at his will.*

The four men stayed in the public house several days without notice. As they went about the city they soon grew appalled at the idolatry, the temple prostitutes, public drunkenness, the disregard for the downtrodden and poor. Here and there they spoke a word about Christ to individuals, prayed together, and waited for the Spirit's leading.

When the Sabbath rolled around, the apostles left the inn to assemble for worship. With Luke leading the way they walked through the city gate and west on the Via Egnatia. Passing through the restricted marginal land, they came to the colonial arch. Luke pointed to the stones' decoration. "This arch symbolizes the dignity of Rome. As we pass under it we leave behind the glory of a 'free city,' a Roman colony."

"Free city," Paul thought, *is an ironic term for this place.* His heart was heavy for what he had seen in Philippi. No wonder the "man of Macedonia" had entreated him to come.

Noting Paul's sadness, Luke spoke cheerfully. "It isn't far now. See the river? It's a fair stream, one of several that find their way to the sea."

"Is that a chapel I see?" asked Silas.

"Yes, you could call it that," Luke answered. "When I asked Euodias about it, she said only women gather there for prayer. They've read the Old Testament in Greek and have come to believe in one God."

"Then it's no synagogue."

"Not without ten men to form a congregation."

As they entered the little building the women were few in number but earnest in devotion, singing one of the psalms, a doxology. Paul and the others took seats and joined in.

When the singing ended, Luke spoke to the women, told

them who Paul was and what their mission was in Macedonia. Paul then sat down in the speaker's chair to proclaim the gospel in Greek, the region's native tongue.

As he surveyed the women before him, Paul thought of other congregations—synagogues full of priests, scribes, Pharisees, and Sadducees. How unlike them were the women before him, God-fearing souls who did not yet know the risen Lord but who were living up to the light they had, assembling to worship the true, invisible God without benefit of rabbi or elder. His heart went out to them.

As Paul spoke about the Old Testament prophecies regarding the Messiah and carefully explained their fulfillment in Jesus from Nazareth, he observed one woman in particular. He sensed that she was particularly drawn to what he was saying. As he talked on, the truth seemed to dawn on her, animating her countenance. Scarcely had he finished explaining God's appearance in the flesh, his death and Resurrection, than she began asking questions.

Realizing that God had opened her heart, Paul inquired as to who she was and learned that she had come from Thyatira—a city some distance away—and that business or marriage, he did not understand which, brought her to Philippi. "My name is Lydia," she told him. "I sell the Phoenician dye and purple fabric."

She was eager to embrace the faith they proclaimed. In a rush of joy she committed herself to the Lord Jesus Christ as her Savior from sin, and she prayed with thanksgiving.

Then Lydia began asking more questions. In answer, the apostles related the accounts of eyewitnesses who had accompanied Jesus. Then they spoke of his teachings and his promises. They explained the rite of baptism, and Lydia requested baptism for herself and her household.

Going down to the banks of the Gangites, the apostles baptized Lydia, the first convert in Europe, and her three daughters. As Silas pronounced the words *I baptize you in the name of the Father, Son, and Holy Ghost,* Paul thanked God for confirming his vision with this token of grace.

After the baptisms the women dispersed, and Lydia, with her family, accompanied Paul and the others back to the city.

"Where are you staying?" she asked. And they told her the name of the public house. "Oh, come to my house," she insisted.

Paul shook his head as did the others, it being the custom to decline the first invitation. As they continued to show reluctance, Lydia stopped in the middle of the road. "If you consider me a believer in the Lord," she said, "come and stay at my house."

Luke seemed to yield. Timothy and Silas looked at Paul as much as to say, "Why not?" So Paul relented. "Very well," he said, "show us the way."

In the days that followed, Paul declared the gospel at every opportunity and was gaining a reputation in Philippi. Those most interested were the women who met every Sabbath by the river. And in Lydia's house he was not without an audience. She plied him with questions, besought him to pray for her and with her, and daily called her children together to be instructed by him.

One Sabbath when they were going to the place of prayer a disheveled girl began following them, at first stealthily, then openly. "I think she's the fortune-teller from the market," Silas said. "See, she's dressed in black."

Lydia glanced over her shoulder. "Aye, she's the one. She not only tells fortunes; that evil spirit in her plays on the ignorance of people—makes them think she can divine. They ask her to solve crimes or find things they've lost— missing persons—and they ask her where fortunes are hidden. The vague answers she gives leave plenty of leeway, so she's never discredited. There are other women who claim such powers, and they make money at it, but this girl is renowned. She's the property of leading citizens, and I can tell you they're getting rich off what she earns."

"Shhh," Timothy cautioned. "What's she saying?"

"These men," the girl cried in an unnatural voice, "are servants of the Most High God who are telling you the way to be saved."

"Do I detect fear in her voice?" Paul asked.

"The devils believe and tremble," Silas remarked under his breath.

"Yes," Luke added, "all the worshipers of idols know there is a supreme God who is Lord of lords, and they fear him."

Timothy looked confused. "I don't like this. What right has she to give such testimony?"

"Perhaps God is prompting her," Luke suggested. "After all, she speaks the truth."

Timothy looked back at the girl. "I think she's mocking us." He tried to stare her down. The girl grinned back at him and kept up the taunting refrain.

As the group continued on their way, the sorceress stayed several paces behind them, proclaiming who they were. People along the road stopped and stared; others began following them.

As they passed under the arch, Luke looked worried. "They look upon her as one who delivers the oracles of God. If she identifies herself with us, people will think we're sorcerers, too. What should we do, Paul?"

"I don't know. It's so like the devil to try to ruffle us, distract us from worshiping the Lord." They had reached the place of prayer. "Come," he said, "let us go into the house of the Lord." As they entered the chapel and closed the door behind them, they could still hear the girl calling after them.

For the next several days, everywhere the apostles went the demon-possessed girl followed, chanting, "These men are servants of the Most High God who are telling you the way to be saved."

Timothy remarked, "Perhaps she does our cause good."

"Hardly," Silas replied. "Satan disguises himself as an angel of light for his own good."

Paul was troubled. "It grieves me to see one so young used of Satan." And although he did not voice it, Paul was incensed that God's truth was being spoken by an evil spirit with purposes unknown to him. This girl was not like Bar-Jesus, the sorcerer in Paphos who had sought to prevent the proconsul, Sergius Paulus, from hearing the Word of God. No, this young woman was declaring God's truth. In Paphos, Paul, filled with the Holy Ghost, had lashed out at Bar-Jesus and cursed him with blindness. But the girl's case was different.

As Paul pondered what he should do, he considered the volatile nature of idolaters. *Like the people of Lystra, the Philippians might quickly turn against us and stone us to death.* So, for the time being he resolved to do nothing until the Lord directed him.

They were approaching a fat man who was listening to the girl and smiling approvingly. "I don't like the looks of this," Luke said. "That man is one of the owners of the girl. He has a part interest in her."

The sorceress gleefully stepped up her ranting and raving, making it impossible for the apostles to hear themselves, much less address the people crowding around them. Paul became so troubled he decided the harassment must end. He turned around, and facing the girl he addressed the unclean spirit. "In the name of Jesus Christ I command you to come out of her!"

In a split second the spirit left the girl's body. The crowd was astonished, amazed at the authority Paul invoked.

Dazed, staring as if awakened from a bad dream, the girl stood frozen in her tracks. Before she recovered, the fat man had summoned some of the other owners, and they rushed forward. Examining the girl's eyes, slapping her face, shoving her about, they realized the spirit had left her. Glaring at the apostles they demanded of her, "Tell us what happened!"

Unsure of what had taken place, she was speechless. But

eyewitnesses were quick to relate what happened.

"Do you know what this means?" the fat man shrieked. "We've lost all revenue from her! She isn't worth the bread she eats!" And with that he flung the girl aside. "Show me the man who did this!"

Someone pointed to Paul. The four men lunged for him, grabbing Silas as well. But not recognizing or not wishing to implicate Timothy and Luke, who appeared to be Greeks, they ignored them. Hustling the pair into the marketplace, they dragged Paul and Silas before the public administrators of justice. The accusers shouted, "These men are Jews and are throwing our city into an uproar by advocating customs unlawful for us Romans to accept or practice."

The crowd, spoiling for excitement, joined in the accusations. "Away with the Jews! Away with the Jews!"

And the fat man said, "What right have they to bring their religion to Philippi?"

"Exactly," answered the justice of the peace. "Take these men to the magistrates!"

A roar of approval went up from the crowd, and as Paul and Silas were pushed and shoved down the street to the governors of the city, the mob surged alongside, their circus mood at fever pitch.

Army officers served as magistrates, and in the tumult they had a hard time hearing the accusations. Paul heard the fat man yelling that the apostles were dangerous men who threatened to turn people from the gods and the laws of Rome.

A magistrate rose to his feet. "We'll get to the bottom of this!" he thundered. "Examine the Jews by scourging!"

Cheers went up from the mob! And the magistrate sat back down, satisfied that the lictor's rod would bring the desired confession. Soldiers pounced on Paul and Silas, tearing the clothes from their bodies. In the crowd, fathers hoisted children onto their shoulders, and boys shinnied up the pillars to gain a better view. Blasphemous epithets were hurled at the apostles as Paul and Silas stood naked in the midst of their tormentors.

Fully aware of the cruelties to come, Paul was trembling. Closing his eyes he tried to fortify himself by thinking of his bleeding Savior, but he was suddenly jerked forward as the soldiers threw him down and bound him to the rack.

With the first blow of the rod Paul bit his lip to keep from screaming and prayed for strength to bear the torture. At every swoosh of the rod he steeled himself, numbly aware that the crowd was counting the blows in unison. Then the lictor's rod started coming down on Silas.

Mercifully, Paul soon lost consciousness. When he revived the crowd had lost count.

An officer called a halt to the whipping. Paul felt a rough hand on his neck pressing for a pulse. "This one's still alive," the soldier shouted.

"So is this one," came a reply. "I'm tired. Let's call it a day."

With that the soldier began unfastening Paul. His head reeling, Paul was pulled to his feet, then dumped face down on a litter. As he was being carried, the rough handling jarred him and made his head ache the more.

The litter was set down at the prison door, and as Paul struggled to his feet, the jailer came running out, his toothless mouth grinning. The magistrate spoke to him threateningly. "Guard these prisoners with your life."

The jailer bowed again and again, assuring the magistrate that the two would never escape his jail. Dragging the apostles past the outer prison, he shoved Paul, then Silas, down the hatch into the dungeon.

At the opening of the hatch, other prisoners roused to see what was happening. Chained to the wall, waiting their fate, they squinted against the unaccustomed light. The jailer secured the torch, then, muttering curses, busied himself putting his latest charges in stocks. First he put Paul's left ankle in one socket, then forced the other leg so far apart the pain shot through Paul's body like a firebrand. The jailer laughed as he clamped shut the stocks. "I guarantee that'll hold you!"

His body so sore he could hardly move, sweat beading his brow, Paul wiped his hand across his face, felt a wetness, and saw it was blood. As the jailer was putting Silas in the stocks, Paul saw the raw welts crisscrossing his friend's body. His back was bloody. *It is not without purpose that we suffer this way. Some good will come of this,* he thought. *It will in some way be for the furtherance of the gospel.*

When the jailer was done, he let out a volley of threats and curses. "I guarantee you'll not get away from me!" he swore. "I'll not suffer a death by torture because of the likes of you escaping!"

With that he left them, taking the torch with him.

In the darkness, Paul could hear the inmates grumbling and groaning, and he understood their pain. He reached for Silas but could not touch him. "Are you all right?" he asked, his voice hoarse and weak.

"We are yet alive, Brother Paul. Thank God."

"True. I do thank him for that, but something more will come from this. The Lord works good from evil. Something good will come from this." Paul's head was swimming. "At least Luke and Timothy were not harmed," he murmured.

"We should pray for them that they won't be charged," Silas said. He began praying aloud, thanking God for survival, interceding for Luke and Timothy. "You have told us, Lord, that we are blessed when people insult us . . . persecute us, and falsely say all kinds of evil against us because of you . . . that we are to rejoice and be glad because great is our reward in heaven . . . we remember the way they persecuted the prophets before us . . . Jeremiah . . . Isaiah . . . Give us the strength and the faith to now count it all joy."

From the pitch of his voice Paul sensed a certain ecstasy exhilarating Silas so that he seemed unmindful of the pain, the thirst, the dungeon. His prayer turned to their fellow prisoners as he entreated God for them.

Paul's body quivered from the pain and the chill of the damp cell. The odor of filth, urine, and mold made his stomach revolt. With conscious effort he tried to recall the words of Jesus that had comforted him before, and knowing Silas needed the same comfort, he spoke them aloud. "Blessed are those who are persecuted because of righteousness, for theirs is the kingdom of heaven."

"Amen," Silas responded.

The words renewed Paul's faith with an upsurge of spirit. He began to rejoice just as he heard something scurrying along the wall. Whatever it was, the other prisoners languishing in the far corner were not alarmed.

"I hear rats," Silas said.

Paul feared rats and felt helpless to defend himself. One of them was scuttling about his foot; he slapped at it until it scurried away.

Breathing a sigh of relief, Paul turned his attention back to prayer. "We should pray for Lydia," he said to Silas, "and for the other women as well."

"And the sorceress."

"Yes, the sorceress . . . and our persecutors as our Lord commanded . . . this jailer."

They prayed aloud, one after the other, back and forth for some time. Paul began to sense the presence of God in the dungeon, and he could hardly continue because so much praise and thanksgiving was welling up within him.

With the pain from groin to ankle excruciating, Paul massaged his leg and prayed for relief or for grace to endure.

"Will they kill us?" Silas asked.

"We are Roman citizens. Already they've violated our rights—bound us, beat us. They'll be afraid once they realize we're citizens."

"It's the mercy of God that we're not dead already."

"True." His head swirling dizzily, Paul tried to concentrate on the sufferings of the Savior, *beaten, spit upon, his body wracked with pain—surely, he understands our pain.* Comforted by the thought, Paul tried to remember the words of the doxology they had sung with the women. "I can't remember the words—"

"To the doxology? I was just thinking of that." As Silas began singing, Paul joined in.

As they sang, one of the prisoners growled, "Don't you know it's the middle of the night?"

Other prisoners rebuked him. "Shut up and listen."

When the doxology ended nothing more was said for a while. Then Silas remarked to Paul, "This must be the way Peter and John felt when they were beaten—so pained they couldn't move. I don't think I ever understood their joy in suffering until now. To think, Paul, we, too, are counted worthy to suffer for his name's sake."

Paul responded quietly, "Hallelujah!" and started singing David's hymn of praise: "I will exalt you, my God the King; I will praise your name for ever and ever."

He found himself singing lustily, and although his pain was not lessened, his joy was increased.

"Let's sing the last of the 'Hallel'," Silas suggested. So they sang from the psalms often chanted during Jewish feasts.

After the Hallel there was Mary's song. But in the midst of the singing came a loud rumbling; the dungeon rocking violently. Paul felt himself jolted once or twice, slamming him this way and that. People were screaming.

But as quickly as it began, the earthquake stopped. Paul was sprawled on the floor, someone on top of him. "Paul?" Silas called.

"You're on top of me, Silas." Still dazed, they groped to untangle themselves. Discovering their legs free from the stocks, they scrambled to their feet. They tried to get their bearings.

Suddenly, the dumbfounded prisoners realized their chains were off and the hatch door wide open. "Wait!" Paul commanded. Overhead they could hear much running about. The distraught jailer, standing above the open hatch, was unsheathing his sword. *He's going to kill himself!* Paul thought and raced to the ladder, yelling, "Don't harm yourself! We are all here!"

The prisoners, respecting Paul, made no move to escape. The jailer called for a torch and in a few minutes was lowering himself into the cell. Falling down before Paul and Silas, he cried out, "Sirs, what must I do to be saved?"

The apostles raised him to his feet and, answering his question, replied, "Believe in the Lord Jesus, and you will be saved—you and your house."

There was much more they had to say to him and, eager to hear, the jailer took them to his quarters on the upper floor. "Wife!" he shouted, "Bring warm water and a towel. They need food!"

Tenderly, the jailer bathed their wounds and treated them with oil. By the time he had finished, a warm supper was set before them. As the apostles ate, they explained more of the gospel to the jailer and his family. As the weight of his sin bore down upon him, the jailer's countenance grew grave.

For several hours Paul and Silas continued teaching him what he needed to know if he was to obey what the Lord commanded. When the jailer fully understood, he believed. "Oh, sirs," he begged, "would you please baptize me and my family?"

The apostles obliged and pronounced the names of the triune God over each soul. For the remainder of the night there was such joy in that house there was little rest.

At daybreak their conversation was interrupted by loud knocking at the gate. Looking down from the window they saw officers waiting impatiently. Paul recognized one of them as the soldier who had beaten Silas so unmercifully. Seeing the jailer's alarm, Paul said, "Come, we'll go with you."

As they reached the gate, the officer spoke. "We have an order," he said, "for the release of the two Jews imprisoned here."

Silas looked at Paul, perplexed "What does this mean?"

The jailer's wife spoke up. "Husband, did you send to the magistrates to plead their case?"

The jailer, disregarding her question, suggested to Paul and Silas, "Perhaps they've heard that you are Roman citizens. One of your friends might have told them. Whatever the reason, the magistrates have ordered that you and Silas be released. Now you can leave. Go in peace."

Paul shook his head and turned to the officers. "They beat us publicly without a trial, even though we are Roman citizens, and threw us into prison. And now do they want to get rid of us quietly? No! Let them come themselves and escort us out."

The officer's face flushed; he turned on his heel and left to report to the magistrates.

As Paul and Silas waited, the jailer was full of talk. "You are generous men," he said. "You could bring action against the magistrates for the indignities done to you. This city could lose its charter if this were known!"

"It is enough that for the public disgrace we've suffered they give us a public discharge acknowledging their injustice," Paul told him. "In that way Philippians will know we are not troublers of the peace as they contend."

"And they will marvel at your grace," the jailer added.

Silas corrected him. "Not our grace but God's."

Paul looked up the street. "Here they come."

The sight of the frantic magistrates running to the prison drew the attention of passersby. The curious Philippians followed them and clustered in the prison yard as the magistrates, demonstrating great remorse, apologized loudly, pleading the mercy of the apostles.

In the morning light the Philippians could plainly see the lacerations from the beatings and, embarrassed by the evidence of their injustice, the magistrates implored the apostles, "Please take your leave." Taking Paul and Silas by the arms they escorted them outside the prison yard, publicly declaring their innocence and urging them not to bring charges.

Onlookers, seeing the respect given the missionaries by the magistrates, looked upon Paul and Silas with awe.

"They're Roman citizens!" people exclaimed.

Satisfied that they were publicly exonerated, the injustice confessed and forgiven, Paul and Silas parted with their escorts and headed for Lydia's house.

Sore and exhausted, they wanted nothing more than the fellowship of their friends. "Luke and Timothy will be there," Silas said. "I can't wait to tell them what God has done!"

STUDY QUESTIONS

1. Why were Luke and Timothy spared persecution?
   A. They had Greek names.
   B. They wore Greek clothing.
   C. They were speaking Greek.

2. What do you think gave Paul and Silas the faith to sing in that dungeon?
   A. Paul had been promised suffering when he was called to preach to the Gentiles.
   B. They remembered the sufferings of Christ.
   C. They remembered the words of Christ promising persecution and instructing believers how to respond.

3. What principle was Paul practicing when he insisted that the officials publicly escort them from the prison?
   A. If they were not publicly vindicated the Philippians would be left with the impression that they were troublemakers.
   B. The fact that the apostle did not press charges to the extent of the law saved the city of Philippi the loss of their charter. This showed the principle of grace.
   C. Believers should not allow themselves to be evil spoken of if they can be vindicated.

Something to Ponder: If persecuted physically could we recall the Scriptures that would enable us to respond as Paul and Silas responded?

14

Gamaliel

IF IT IS FROM GOD . . . YOU WILL ONLY FIND YOURSELVES
FIGHTING AGAINST GOD.

Scripture: Acts 5:39; 21:27–22:24

Gamaliel tied the thongs around the heavy scroll and put it back in the cabinet. His grandfather's library was his treasure, and it pleased him to know that he would pass it on to his grandson in the sure knowledge that he, too, would treasure it.

What a promising student his namesake was. Far excelling others his age in the study of religion, there was every reason to believe that he would become a scholar in the tradition of his grandfather and great-grandfather, Hillel. Gamaliel anticipated that when the boy made his mark the Jewish academics would find it necessary to distinguish between himself and his grandson with some such designation as Gamaliel the Elder or Gamaliel the Less. Whether his grandson would ever be called *Rabban*, as he was called, remained to be seen. Gamaliel was the only man to have been given that title meaning "our master, our great one," but he knew that in time there would be others.

Under Gamaliel's tutelage there had once been another promising student, a young man from Tarsus who outstripped every scholar he had ever taught the Law and classics. *If ever I had a protégé, it was Saul,* he said, and he thought of the years he had spent encouraging him in learning and in zeal. Seeing Saul's potential, he was grooming him for a judgeship on the Sanhedrin, that august body of seventy

Jewish elders who tried cases involving the Law. *Yes, Saul of Tarsus might also have become a Rabban,* he told himself. *If only he had not become an apostate.*

Gamaliel heaved a sigh and walked to the window that gave a view of the Temple courtyard. As much as he deplored Saul's defection, his passion for truth caused him to acknowledge doubts in his own mind. For several years he had followed the activities of Paul, as he now called himself, and wrestled with the issues that separated them.

Perhaps of secondary importance was Paul's acceptance of Gentiles—eating, staying in their homes, preaching a message that included them. In the legalistic code of Gamaliel's Pharisaism only Jews were subjects of God's favor. Yet Gamaliel had long observed from the books of the Law that Gentiles, too, were in the mind of God. *Did he not send Jonah to the Ninevites—Daniel to the Babylonians?* he asked himself. *Was the nation Israel not supposed to set an example among the peoples of the world to attract the Gentiles to God?*

The second issue concerned him profoundly. It was the matter of Resurrection. His first encounter with the apostles of Jesus involved the preaching of the Nazarene's Resurrection. The followers of the Way were firmly convinced that their rabbi rose from the dead in the same body in which he was buried. And Gamaliel admitted that in Jerusalem shortly after the Crucifixion even the Sanhedrin was not unmindful of the facts in the case. When three thousand Jews became followers of the Nazarene it was because his Resurrection was verified by many witnesses. Gamaliel could not shake the fact that at that time Jesus' Resurrection was a matter of public knowledge. But he understood why the religious establishment discredited the Nazarene. For members of the Sanhedrin to acknowledge his Resurrection would cost them their political power and prestige.

Even so the conflict remained within himself. As a Pharisee, Gamaliel was firmly convinced that everyone would rise from the dead as taught in the Law. *Yet, upon hearing that a man is raised from the dead, we Pharisees were the first to refute it.* He shook his head. *I, for instance, would like to know where this Jesus is now. They say he ascended, but did he? Is there any evidence that he is yet alive? These are the questions we should be asking.* After all the hard-fought battles with the Sadducees, who disbelieved in anything supernatural, it seemed inconsistent to him that Pharisees would dismiss the report of a resurrection instead of pursuing the matter to its proper conclusion.

That inconsistency was uppermost in his mind the day he was called in on a case involving two Galileans charged with preaching the message of the Way in the Temple. So disturbed was he by his own misgivings, Gamaliel advised the Sanhedrin, "Men of Israel, consider carefully what you intend to do to these men." Then he cited the cases of two leaders who had led uprisings. In each case the popular movements had come to naught. "Therefore," he concluded, "in the present case I advise you: Leave these men alone! Let them go! For if their purpose or activity is of human origin, it will fail. But if it is from God, you will not be able to stop these men; you will only find yourselves fighting against God."

The satisfaction he felt when they followed his advice was one thing, but in the intervening years he was made uncomfortable by the wildfire spread of Christianity. *I wonder how many of the Sanhedrin remember my logic that day in court? Are they troubled as I am that the movement has not failed? Well, of course they are troubled—they're doing everything they can to stop the spread—but are they troubled that we may be wrong?*

As Gamaliel lay down to sleep, his own words haunted him, "If it is from God, you will not be able to stop these men; you will only find yourselves fighting against God."

The next day Gamaliel heard encouraging news. A student told him that Saul of Tarsus was in town with his head shaved. That could mean only one thing, he had taken a vow of purification. *So, he has not rejected Jewish vows,* Gamaliel decided. *Has he seen the error of his ways?* he wondered.

But whatever hopes he had that his protégé was returning to Pharisaism were dashed by the next day's events. A great commotion was going on in the Temple, and Gamaliel walked outside where he might hear what was happening. An excited crowd was swarming the courtyard when someone came out the Temple door and shouted, "Men of Israel, help us! This is the man who teaches all people everywhere against our people and our Law and this place. And besides, he has brought Greeks into the Temple area and defiled this holy place."

"Who is it?" he asked, knowing in his heart it was Saul, but his words were lost in the confusion.

Men dashed inside to assist in the removal of the offender as more and more people were pouring into the courtyard from all directions. As the mob came dragging its victim through the door, Gamaliel glimpsed the bleeding face of Saul of Tarsus. People were beating him about the head, kicking him. *Oh, no!* Gamaliel groaned. *Where are the soldiers?*

About that time he saw red-cloaked troops racing across the courtyard. "Here come the troops!" someone shouted, but the rioters kept hitting Saul.

The Roman commander forced his way to the bleeding man, shouting, "Who is this man? What's he done?"

The response was utter confusion as people shouted one thing and another. Seeing he could not get to the bottom of the matter, the officer arrested the victim and had him bound hand and foot. Ordering the soldiers, he shouted, "Take the prisoner to the fortress!"

As they struggled up the barrack steps the mob rushed at Paul savagely, grabbing him by the arms and legs, trying to pull him apart. Quickly the guards wrested him from them, and lifting the prisoner above their heads, they carried him. "Away with him! Away with him!" the crowd chanted.

When Paul was about to be taken inside the Antonia Fortress, Gamaliel saw them stop and put him down. There was some discussion, and then Paul stood on the steps before the crowd waiting as if to speak. Gamaliel pushed his way through the crowd to get closer.

From the wall of the portico he could hear Paul speaking in Aramaic. "Brothers and fathers, listen now to my defense."

Gamaliel winced at the sound of his voice. Of all Paul's gifts, oratory was not one of them.

"I am a Jew," he heard him say, "born in the city of Tarsus of Cilicia, but brought up in this city. Under Gamaliel I was thoroughly trained in the law of our fathers and was just as zealous for God as any of you are today. I persecuted the followers of this Way to their death, arresting both men and women and throwing them into prison, as also the high priest and all the council can testify."

Gamaliel could see Paul clearly. He showed the marks of deprivation: bandy-legged from floggings, his once fair skin weatherbeaten, his body thin and poorly clad. *I would not have known him*, Gamaliel thought, *except for the intensity of his eyes. He burns with zeal as he always has.*

Paul's thin voice rasped on. "I even obtained letters from the Council to their brothers in Damascus and went there to bring these people as prisoners to Jerusalem to be punished."

Gamaliel remembered the orders when they were written for Saul.

"About noon," he continued, "as I came near Damascus, suddenly a bright light from heaven flashed around me. I fell to the ground and heard a voice say to me, 'Saul! Saul! Why do you persecute me?'

" 'Who are you, Lord?' I asked.

" 'I am Jesus of Nazareth, whom you are persecuting,' the voice replied."

Gamaliel felt the blood rush to his head. He could not believe his ears! *He's saying he heard this Jesus speak! Can it be true?* His eyes, riveted on the face of the suffering man, saw nothing there to make him doubt. *Saul is the same principled man I knew. No, he's not lying.*

"My companions saw the light," he was saying, "but did not understand the voice of him who was speaking to me.

" 'What shall I do, Lord?' I asked.

" 'Get up,' the Lord said, 'and go into Damascus. There you will be told all that you have been assigned to do.' My companions led me by the hand into Damascus, because the brilliance of the light had blinded me."

Blinded him, Gamaliel questioned. *He cannot be lying, there are too many details—*

"A man named Ananias came to see me. He was a devout observer of the Law and highly respected by all the Jews living there. He stood beside me and said, 'Brother Saul, receive your sight!' And at that very moment I was able to see him.

"Then Ananias said, 'The God of our fathers has chosen you to know his will and to see the Righteous One and to hear words from his mouth. You will be his witness to all people of what you have seen and heard. And now what are you waiting for? Get up, be baptized, and wash your sins away, calling on his name.' "

So that is it, thought Gamaliel. Perspiration was trickling down his face. *This Jesus is God to him.* He shook his head. *Can it be?* He leaned forward to catch every word.

"When I returned to Jerusalem and was praying at the Temple, I fell into a trance and saw the Lord speaking. 'Quick!' he said to me. 'Leave Jerusalem immediately, because they will not accept your testimony about me.' "

That's true, Gamaliel said to himself. *The Sanhedrin had plans to kill him.*

" 'Lord,' I replied, 'these men know that I went from one synagogue to another to imprison and beat those who believe in you. And when the blood of your martyr Stephen was shed, I stood there giving my approval and guarding the clothes of those who were killing him.' "

Gamaliel remembered the stoning, although he had not personally witnessed it.

"Then the Lord said to me, 'Go; I will send you far away to the Gentiles.' "

Gamaliel's jaw tightened. *Can it be that God sent this Pharisee of the Pharisees to Gentiles?*

The crowd broke into an uproar. "Rid the earth of him! He's not fit to live!" they shouted. Scooping up handfuls of dust they threw it and their cloaks into the air, protesting the sacrilege. Soldiers in ranks held back the mob gone mad as the commander ordered the prisoner taken into the fortress.

They'll flog him, Gamaliel thought and turned away, unable to bear the sight.

That night the Rabban could not sleep. As he paced the floor he could not deny that his questions had been answered. *Saul of Tarsus would not lie and suffer the consequences he has endured. He truly believes he encountered Jesus on the way to Damascus.*

Gamaliel tried to think of every possible explanation. *Was the encounter a delusion—a trick of the noonday sun? Or, angry as he was, did he suffer apoplexy? Perhaps too much study had made him mad.* All night he wrestled with his thoughts, but always he came back to the nagging truth—Saul of Tarsus believed he met the ascended Jesus, and it had changed his life dramatically.

Knowing the truth, Gamaliel knew it called for a decision. Neutrality was not an option. He weighed the consequences. *To commit myself to Jesus as Lord will mean what it meant to Saul—loss of position and certain persecution. At my age,* he reasoned, *I would soon die.*

He got up and, going to the window, watched the day dawn. *Perhaps I can personally acknowledge him yet maintain my position as Joseph and Nicodemus have done.* But he could not bring himself to be secretive.

Gamaliel's grandson was coming in the gate. A scroll under his arm, hurrying as he always was, his robe billowed out behind him. He was a handsome boy with dark eyes and long, curly prayer locks.

If I go the way of the Nazarene, the boy will be disgraced. And it was Gamaliel's weakness for the boy that decided the matter for him. *I cannot,* he said. *I owe my grandson the heritage.*

The youth came bouncing up the stairs two at a time. "Grandfather," he called out and burst in the room. "Did you hear about the apostate? He's a Roman citizen and that saved his hide yesterday."

"Indeed."

"The Sanhedrin has been called to question him. Will you be going?"

"I think not."

"They could use your advice."

It was ironic that his grandson should say just that, for ringing in Gamaliel's ears was the advice he had once given: *If it is of God . . . you will only find yourselves fighting against God.*

"I think you should go," the grandson insisted. "They'll need your help if they convict him."

He could not refuse the urgency of the younger Gamaliel. "Very well. Hand me my cane."

STUDY QUESTIONS

1. In the student-teacher relationship of Gamaliel and Paul, what possibilities were presented?
   A. Paul learned the Hebrew Scriptures from Gamaliel and that served him well later on.
   B. Paul gained the skills of good study habits, debate, and persuasian under Gamaliel, skills the Lord used.
   C. Paul's education in the classics under Gamaliel gave him the credentials he needed to command the attention of the Greeks.

2. What do you think kept Gamaliel from accepting the gift of faith?
    A. Pride.
    B. Spiritual blindness.
    C. An evil heart of unbelief.

3. What inconsistencies do you find in Gamaliel?
    A. After giving advice about Peter and John ("If this is not of God nothing will come of it, if it is of God we don't want to fight against it"), he lived to see the remarkable spread of Christianity, yet did not disapprove the persecution of Christians nor accept Christ.
    B. As a Pharisee he believed in resurrection, yet when the evidences of Christ's resurrection became public knowledge, he did not embrace the truth.
    C. A scholar thoroughly acquainted with Old Testament prophecies, he could not fail to see their fulfillment in Jesus of Nazareth.

Something to Ponder: There are more people who reject the gift of faith than those who receive it. How can we make the gift more attractive?